Dog Showing
for Beginners

Lynn Hall

HOWELL
BOOK HOUSE
New York

Howell Book House
Macmillan General Reference
A Simon & Schuster Macmillan Company
1633 Broadway
New York, NY 10019-6785

MACMILLAN is a registered trademark of Macmillan, Inc.

Library of Congress Cataloging-in-Publication Data

Hall, Lynn.
    Dog showing for beginners / by Lynn Hall.
        p.   cm.
    ISBN 0-87605-408-4
    1. Dogs—Showing.   2. Dog shows.   I. Title.
SF425.H33   1994
636.7′0888—dc20   94-1550
                                                     CIP

Manufactured in the United States of America

10   9   8   7   6   5   4   3

Contents

Why a Survivors' Handbook?

WHY, YOU ASK. Is this a hobby you're getting yourself into, or open warfare? A jungle out there, a dog-eat-dog world? End of clichés. End of scare tactics.

Yes, it's a hobby. Yes, it's all those other things, too. And it has a high dropout rate. The purpose of this book is to help you get maximum enjoyment out of showing your dog, in the hope that you too won't become a dropout.

This is not intended to be an in-depth treatise on any one aspect of showing dogs, but a realistic overview of the sport, of what you can expect. Forewarned is forearmed.

When I was nineteen I discovered dog shows, and announced to my dismayed parents that I'd found my niche in the world. I took a job as a professional handler's assistant, thinking I was on my way to the perfect career—professional handling.

The job lasted three days. That was when I learned that the job description included cleaning runs, combing mats, and compromising my ethics. Cleaning runs and combing mats I was prepared for, even eager for.

At number three, I drew the line.

In the decades since I've come to accept the bad sides of the dog show world and even to find ways around them. But it was a long process of idealism warring with reality.

It took time to find the balance that now allows me to show my own dogs, spend most weekends at shows, get my share of the wins on a level that satisfies me and thoroughly and genuinely enjoy this hobby.

It can be done. My hope, in writing this book, is to help you past the beginner stage and on to your own balance, your own style of loving a sport with built-in pitfalls.

1

Do I Really Want to Do This?

YOU'RE STANDING ON THE BRINK. You've just been watching the annual Westminster spectacle on television and you're drawn to the glitz and excitement of the dog show world.

Or, you've just spent a Sunday visiting your own local annual dog show—it's the third year you've gone and watched—and the feeling growing inside you makes you want to be part of this world.

Or, you've just bought a purebred puppy from a renowned breeder who tells you the pup is good enough to show, and you're tempted to give it a try.

Or maybe owning a show dog is a deep old dream you've held since childhood.

Looking in from the outside, it all seems a little scary. Here are hundreds of people who know exactly what they're doing, hundreds of beautiful dogs attached to competent-looking handlers, and snatches of a foreign language in the air.

"Space cadet dumped me to the bred-by and put the pig up Best Op for a four-point major. He's not doing our specialty, he can kiss that one good-bye, the blind old. . . ."

Like any hobby group or subculture or whatever the dog show world is, it can seem intimidating to the newcomer. But every one of those confident-looking exhibitors started as a glassy-eyed novice, and if they can make it, you can. Get a good grip on this book and we'll tackle it together.

Why do people show dogs? There are lots of sound reasons, a few neurotic reasons, too, but mostly good ones. Almost everyone begins with a genuine love for dogs or for a specific breed. Dogs excite us. A beautiful dog is a thrill to watch, especially after we know enough to appreciate it. Dogs are not only beautiful, they are loving and they adore us. We eat it up.

Dogs offer an outlet for our need to control. A dog breeder is in a God-position. We make decisions about life and death, birth and euthanasia, feeding, grooming, and exercising. It's all work, of course, but it's work in which we are in complete control. That feels good, especially if we have little control over people and events around us at work or in the family.

A show dog is in many ways an ego extension. We own the dog, the dog is part of our self-image. We may be short and fat and homely, but we own a Greyhound! For many people, owning a power dog is owning power. Controlling an animal others may fear gives us a wonderful rush.

Most people must give affection in huge quantities, and have no appropriate humans in their lives for channeling those feelings. Dogs are perfect absorbers and returners of love.

For many, dogs provide a visual and tactile pleasure. Stroking a silky, woolly, or sleek hard coat provides sensual pleasure. Feasting our eyes on rich coat color or brilliant markings nourishes our hunger for beauty. There's no need to analyze it, it's there to be enjoyed.

If we own beautiful dogs, the next logical step is to want them to be seen and admired in public. Going into a show ring and coming out with a blue ribbon serves as proof to the world that we, the dog and us, are a bit superior. It's human nature.

Being competitive is also human nature. We fight wars, we beat each other out for promotions on the job, we gloat over our new cars that outshine the neighbors' less-new cars. We participate in

Often the best part of your dog show weekend is the quiet time, just you and your dog. Bonding can be particularly intense at that time.

sports to prove our superiority. We dress competitively. We some-times steal one another's wives and husbands to see if we can.

Around dog shows you'll often hear people say, "We don't care whether we win or not, we just show for the fun of it." Don't believe it! Winning is fun. Winning is a high that equals any chem-ical high ever invented. Losing is not fun, it's just a long day, a long drive, and a lot of work capped by disappointment. Most people lose more than they win, but one good win can keep us afloat through a lot of losses.

Some like to say, "We enter dog shows to get the judge's opinion." I don't buy that one, either. If the judge's opinion is that our dog is fourth-best in a class of four, we don't want that opinion. We want the win. We want the elation of sailing out of the ring with that blue or purple scrap of fabric. We want the job of being a gracious winner at ringside, followed by the whooping elation all the way home.

That's why we show dogs.

Dog Show Dropouts

There is a high drop-out rate among dog show exhibitors. People get in, stay a year or two, and drop out. Why? Several reasons. Lots of people are tasters, not eaters. They got into dogs for a taste of the dog show world, and having tasted, moved on to other hobbies. Sometimes the excuse is that "dog shows are so political we just got sick of it," but the real reason is more apt to be lack of dedication to dogs.

Some people get in for the kids, and get out when the kids are grown and gone, or when the kids discover sex, cars, true love, and better ways to spend their weekends than being dragged to dog shows with Mom and Dad.

Some people drop out because the family splits, or unemploy-ment cuts into the budget, or their parents' terminal illness drains them of time and money. They often drop back in later, when life smooths out a little.

Others drop out because they collide with the unsavory facts of dog show life and can't deal with them any other way. Yes, there are immoral participants in the dog sport. Yes, there are political goings-on going on sometimes. Yes, competitors can get nasty, especially if you're beating them. People looking for a reason to quit showing can always find a noble one. "Dog shows are too crooked for me." They tend to ignore the other, equally valid side of the picture; the good judges, the hard-working breeders, the basic sense of fairness that underscores the majority of dogfolks' relationships with one another.

Probably the greatest underlying cause for dropping out is unrealistic expectations. So many beginners jump into showing because they've bought a purebred dog with a "pedigree as long as your arm, and it's got three champions on it." Often the dog is pet quality, no more. Most pedigrees have at least a few champions; this isn't a realistic basis for assuming that the dog in question is champion quality himself. A proud owner goes to a few local shows, finds himself at the bottom of every class, is perhaps told by other exhibitors that his dog is not show quality, and that's the end of the dog show hobby.

Many others in this situation, of course, keep the first dog as a pet and buy a better one to continue showing.

An often overlooked fact of life is that a dog show is not a local pet show, where any purebred dog is going to stand out. Even small shows are serious competitions in which the dogs come from breeders who have been working for years to produce superior dogs, and competitors have been at it a long time.

It's simply unrealistic to expect to go into competition with a dog from an undistinguished background, knowing nothing about training or grooming or what class to enter, and expect to win Best In Show over a thousand or two thousand competitors. Yet this is exactly what many newcomers do hope and expect. It's not a realistic dream and when it fails to happen, people go sour.

You don't need to make this mistake. Educate yourself. Treat the sport of showing dogs with the same respect you'd treat any other sport and go through the learning process before you build up expectations of taking the world by storm.

You wouldn't expect to win Wimbledon after four tennis lessons, but you can dream of winning big after you've learned and practiced and polished, and earned the right to dream big.

*   *   *

Do you really want to get into this? Here are some pros and cons to weigh on the balance scale:

The Costs

What will it all cost? First, there is the cost of a dog good enough to win. Prices vary from breed to breed, but you should expect to pay between $500 and $1,000 for a likely puppy, more than that for a show-worthy young adult. A finished champion with a proven win record can cost much more, sometimes $20,000 to $50,000, though these sales aren't as common in dogs as they are in horses. In the more populous breeds you might find a show-quality puppy for less than $500. There are no hard and fast rules.

Equipment: A crate is a basic necessity, $20 to $80 depending on size and type. The crate is where the dog rests at the show when not being shown, what he rides in, and often his bed at home.

For most breeds, a grooming table is also a necessity. It's your work space at the show and can double as picnic table and "stuff-dumping" surface, but mostly it's for grooming your dog just before he goes into the ring. A table with grooming arm will run about $80.

Grooming equipment: if your breed requires electric clippers, count on around $80 plus blades. Combs, brushes, scissors, and nail clippers are all small items, necessary but not big-ticket purchases.

A little asking around should put you in touch with one of the good wholesale kennel supply catalogs from which all of the necessities mentioned here can be ordered.

Show entry fees: These keep going up by gradual steps. Presently they are averaging about $20. Although they can add up over time, they aren't exorbitant compared to other competition hobbies. You only enter one class at any one dog show, so your entries for a two-show weekend will be around $40. The average serious exhibitor might go to twenty show weekends each year. Showing one dog, that would be around $800 a year in entries.

Travel expenses: these would of course depend on how many shows you attend, how far from home you travel, and whether you stay in motels. If you live near a large city you may be able to find all the shows you want within easy driving distance, so that you can finish your champion without ever having to pay for motel rooms. If you don't live near a major metropolitan area, be prepared to travel some distance to find the shows you need, and be prepared to pay the cost.

If you have fallen in love with a rare breed, you may discover that there is no competition in your area, and that if you hope to finish your dog's championship you'll have to go where there are others of the same breed. This can mean more traveling than you bargained for.

You can judge a person's degree of dedication to dog shows by what he drives. The beginner has the family sedan or hatchback, the semiserious a wagon or minivan. Vans, camper-vans, motor homes of all sizes, trailers, motor homes pulling trailers, and vans pulling trailers—these indicate exhibitors for whom dog shows have become the center of their lives, as profession or addictive hobby or any combination.

So be prepared. You too may find yourself at the car dealer's, taking that upward step into serious dogdom.

Besides money-costs there are time-costs to be considered. Showing dogs is addictive, and most people who start small find themselves going more and more often, traveling farther, and shaving work time on Fridays and Mondays for the show trips. If your job allows for this and you can afford it, fine. If not, you may find yourself driving all night Friday to get to Saturday's show site, then arriving home at 2:00 A.M. Monday in order to get to work on time. This is not a restful weekend, and if it happens too often it can affect your production at work.

If dog shows are a family hobby, fine. If not, the time they demand may be resented by other family members. Some couples work it out amicably: while she goes showing, he goes fishing. Or while he goes to the dog show she has a lazy weekend at home not having to watch his stupid football games. One couple I know, with a small child, worked out this system: Wife and dogs were delivered to the show site, then husband and son left for the nearest zoo or amusement park, getting back to the show site in time to cheer Mom on in the Groups or console her on the trip home.

If you have a camper, trailer, or RV, dog show weekends can be fun and reasonably comfortable for the whole family because there is a place to watch television, read, nap, or socialize while the show-addicted family member is doing his or her thing.

Some families make miniholidays out of show weekends, with the noninvolved family members holing up in a nearby motel with pool and other recreational facilities for the kids.

These are the major costs you will pay for your dog showing hobby; the initial expense of dog and equipment, the ongoing costs of entry fees, gas, motels or RV equipment, and the expenditure of time that might otherwise be spent on family, home chores, work, or on other forms of recreation.

Only you can decide how much is too much for you.

The Gains

On the credit side, what will you get out of it? For one thing, excitement. Any competition is exciting. You prepare, you dream, you work and practice and polish yourself and your dog, then you go forth into competition. Stomach muscles clench, mouths go dry, pulses pound. It's exciting. And most of us need more of that in our lives.

New friends. New enemies. You'll find both, and both can be equally stimulating. There are wonderful people in the dog show world. With luck you'll buy your first dog from one of them, or at least make contact early on with someone who will be kind and helpful and who will evolve into a friend.

There are rotten people, too, and you're bound to bump up against a few of them. If you keep your sense of perspective and humor, you can survive the slings and arrows and you'll find that the little acrimonies make fodder for the after-show phone reports with the friends who dislike the same people you dislike, and who love to hear about the gossip at ringside.

The same drive for drama that makes some people soap opera addicts is also at work in the dog world. Old animosities fester, newcomers are recruited into long-standing feuds between rival breeders, and on it goes. If you can keep your perspective and take none of it too seriously, it can be an endlessly fascinating fireworks display of human emotion.

If you're interested in travel and sight-seeing, dog shows can add purpose and direction; your breed's national specialty is being held in Houston this year? Fine. You arrange time off from work and make a holiday out of it.

Another advantage that dog shows can add to your life is the chance to excel, the chance to study a new field and become expert, at least expert enough to impress the gang at work, and that's always fun. If yours is a groomed breed, you can derive deep satisfaction from learning to do first an adequate job of show grooming, and then a good job, and finally an excellent job that other newcomers admire you for. We all love to be admired; this is a way to earn it.

For most of us hard-core dog people, our entire social life gradually becomes centered on our doggy friends. We join a local kennel club and maybe a specialty club (for one breed only), and from these groups and the other exhibitors in our breed whom we gradually get to know at ringside comes our social structure. Many of us live somewhat isolated lives and we would be truly lonely if we didn't have kennel club meetings, training class on Monday nights, fun matches, and shows most weekends.

It's a group to belong to—no better than any other group, no worse, but a group with whom we have a strong bond in common. It's a good feeling.

But for me and for most dog show enthusiasts, the best part of it all is the closeness we feel with our dogs as we hit the highway on a sunny Friday afternoon heading toward the show we've been dreaming about all month; as we finally sail into the ring; as we accept the ribbon; as we drive home in the glow of a good win, under a good judge, against tough competition. It's a partnership with a beautiful animal whom we love and who loves us. It's wonderful!

Now you've looked at the major pros and cons. Do you want to do this?

If so, stick with me and we'll go through this novice stuff together.

This Collie puppy is clearly a quality youngster, with obvious promise. His owner would be justified in being eager to start his career at the first available fun match.

2

Finding the Right Breed, Breeder and Dog

If YOU'RE STANDING smack in the middle of square one, with no commitment yet to a dog or even a specific breed, you're still in a position to make wise choices. Most people don't use much wisdom in selecting a breed, but perhaps the visceral response we have to that one special look, that one special dog, is a truer guide than good sense.

Selecting our breed is like selecting a mate. We may pass up a flock of steady fellows that Mom would have loved as a son-in-law, and then fall inexplicably in love with the least likely candidate. We may live to regret that choice, but we'd probably regret even more compromising and settling for something less than the one who made our hearts go pitty-pat.

Let's give a moment of practical thought to the things that should be considered in choosing a breed. Then, if you want to go ahead and fall in love with the wrong one, it'll be off my conscience.

Size

The rule of thumb here is obvious though not necessarily valid; big dogs don't do well in city apartments, tiny dogs do. But maybe you are a city cliff-dweller with a passion for magnificently large dogs. Or you might be a country person who happens to love tiny dogs with long, flowing coats.

Size may be less important than energy level. Some giant breeds are quiet, passive animals that can be perfectly content in an apartment. Breeds like German Shepherd Dogs and Dalmatians, although smaller than Irish Wolfhounds, have a higher energy level and a compelling need for action, which, if thwarted, can lead to destructive and dangerous behavior.

It is important, though, that you are physically able to control and dominate your dog. If you are small and slight and think you're in love with Alaskan Malamutes because of their appearance, try looking at smaller dogs of a similar general type. Norwegian Elkhounds and Keeshonden might give you the same visual pleasure on a much more controllable scale.

If you love tiny dogs but have wildly athletic children, look for a small but heavy-boned breed rather than something fragile. Corgis are wonderful in that situation, as well as some of the short-legged terrier breeds.

Temperament

If you have a strong urge to love and be loved by your dog, you may be disappointed if you buy an aloof breed, one that disappears at every opportunity and only comes to you by bodily force.

If you have an agile mind and don't suffer human fools gladly, you're not likely to be satisfied with a blockheaded dog, especially when there are bright breeds eager to learn and to earn your praise. Watching obedience classes can tell you more about a breed's mental abilities than just asking breeders' opinions.

It's a smorgasbord out there. You don't have to grab the first breed that comes to mind, or the breed you had when you were a kid, or the breed somebody at work has and brags about constantly. There are more than 130 AKC-recognized breeds, and dozens more outside the limits of the AKC, hundreds more if you consider all the foreign breeds, but let's keep it practical. The point is, with some research in dog books, some visits to dog shows, and a whole lot of talking with people who own the ones you're interested in, you should be able to find the breed tailor-made for you.

The catch here is that it's sometimes hard to find out the drawbacks in a breed beforehand. People who own them probably love them and either can't see the drawbacks, don't consider them important, or gloss over them as a small price to pay for the advantages. It's like asking a new car owner if he's happy with his car. Who is going to admit he made a dumb choice?

So it pays to ask pointed questions. Ask them of a variety of people, then distill the probable truth from all you've heard. Remember, too, dogs within a breed can vary from bloodline to bloodline: one owner telling you his dog has a lovely temperament and another telling you not to have this breed in a home with children may both be telling you the truth as they know it from their experiences.

What Motivates Our Choices

We choose our breeds as we do because our dogs are a visible extension of our perceptions of ourselves and of our fantasies. My fantasies are visions of myself in an English country cottage with masses of flowers outside and rolling hills crisscrossed with stone walls. My breeds? Bedlington Terriers, Collies, English Cockers.

We choose for physical accommodation. I'm small. I don't enjoy being knocked silly by large, happy sporting breeds. I was afraid to play volleyball in high school for fear of other people's elbows in my face. I love breeds I can control easily with a light touch on the lead. Collies, though large, are lightfooted, floaty dogs who follow at your side with minimal lead control. Conversely, I want a dog big enough to keep me warm in bed on a cold night without fear of my rolling over and squashing it. I want an armful to hug and a neck big enough to cry into when all the world is lining up to spit upon my shoe.

I tend to choose my dogs for beautiful color. I buy cars that way, too, but that's a different story and one I'm ashamed to go into. I think "signature color" is the current phrase. My signature color is blue. Blue Bedlingtons, blue merle Collies, blue roan English Cockers. I've never kept a nonblue vehicle more than two years. Who knows why we're drawn to certain color families, maybe because of our own coloring and what looks good on us. Sweaters, dogs, cars . . . I had a friend who loved black. Black everything. Her partner loved big. Big everything. They walked into their first dog show, saw their first Newfoundland, and bingo, that was it.

Coats and Grooming

Long coat versus smooth, wiry, woolly, or silky: again, if we were to be practical we'd all have shorthaired dogs, but would life be worth living? For whatever our individual reasons, we are pleased by a particular kind of coat, and for most of us, if that coat requires work to maintain, it's worth it. For me, that hour or so after supper, grooming dogs in the quiet kennel with the TV for company and the day's work behind me, is the best part of the day. It's relaxing, it probably does wonders for the blood pressure, and it gives bone-deep pleasure. I'm a connoisseur polishing my rare and valuable collection, but these aren't cold artifacts, they are warm, loving creatures who submit to having their ears tweezed and their armpits combed because they enjoy my attention.

So while I know that the practical advice I'm supposed to be offering here is to consider your work schedule and not to take on a breed needing lots of grooming if you don't have time to do it, I'm not convinced that that's always the best advice. Most people can make time if they want to. You may not want to, and that's fine, too. Be guided by your instincts, not mine.

Instincts. Look for a breed that pleases you instinctively. It may be a subconscious remembrance from childhood, a declaration of your individual self as you perceive it or want others to perceive it. Whatever the reason, you will probably be happier longer with a love match than with a practical choice.

Actively Looking

Next comes researching the breed of your choice. You've probably already met a few breeders, maybe you've been offered a puppy from an upcoming litter, maybe you think this breeder would be fine

14

to buy from. And maybe you'd be right, but if you want to avoid the most common beginner errors, now is the time to step back, sit on your checkbook for a while, and do your homework.

Every breed has genetic problems, some more than others. These might include hip dysplasia, progressive retinal atrophy, epilepsy, cataracts, or whatever. The more common the breed, the more numerous its problems generally. But it's probably safe to say that every breed has something of an inherited nature that buyers need to know about before they buy. Ask around. Some breeders may try to tell you, nah, nothing to worry about in this breed. Keep on truckin', keep on asking. Find out what the common genetic problems are in your chosen breed, find out what testing is possible for that defect, find out who the breeders are who talk about it openly and are careful not to breed from dogs who have it.

One source of information about your chosen breed can be the breed's parent club. The club contact person's name and address can be obtained from the American Kennel Club. A word of caution here: not all parent clubs are willing to admit to genetic problems in their breed. If key people in that club happen to have a bloodline loaded with whichever besetting defect that breed is heir to, those people may well be able to suppress the facts on that point. *Caveat emptor.*

A good way to research your breed might be with a current copy of a magazine such as *Dog World* or *Dog Fancy,* and just do a telephone survey of everyone advertising dogs for sale in its classified columns. These magazine ads are the most common entrée into purebred dogs. Present yourself as just what you are, a potential buyer just looking for now, trying to learn more about the breed. Most advertisers will be happy to talk your ear off. It's their favorite topic and you are at least a potential buyer.

Thus the research stage slips into the shopping-around stage, but the longer you can hold off and the more different viewpoints you can garner, the better your final decision is likely to be, and the more comfortable you'll feel with it.

You can, of course, write letters to all these advertisers, too, but you're less likely to get replies and you may come off looking like a bad risk for a show puppy. If you can't or won't pay for a phone call, will you be able to afford show entries and travel expenses and good quality dog food and all the rest of it? Will you pay for your puppy with a rubber check? These things occur to breeders, and since the better dogs come from the better breeders and are usually in demand, it's a good idea to make the best first impression you can.

I tend not to answer inquiries that come in dime store envelopes with pencil-printed addresses, letters on torn segments of notebook paper or letters full of misspellings and bad grammar. Although I may be passing up an occasional rough diamond, it seems much more likely that these are not people who will pay substantial prices for quality animals and then do justice to them.

Talking to Breeders

When you start shopping in earnest for that first show puppy, you might be better off shopping for the right breeder rather than for an individual dog. An honest, knowledgeable, successful show breeder who takes a liking to you is your best hope for early success in the show ring. The part about taking a liking to you is the key, here. If you begin the acquaintance by offending or making a bad impression it's unlikely that this breeder is going to want to sell you a puppy.

How to offend a breeder: Opening questions like, "How much are you asking for your dogs?" can do it. Putting price at the top of your priority list will raise red warning flags in the breeder's mind. Good breeders are continually on guard against incipient puppy millers, investor-types who are getting into the breed to make a quick buck, usually to the detriment of the dogs. The popular breeds are especially vulnerable to canine carpetbaggers, and you don't want to get slotted into that category two seconds into your first phone call.

"Hi, I heard you had some dogs you was wanting to get rid of."

"Are you the lady that's got those Bredlinger, Bredington, Beddingham, those terrier things?"

"Hello, I'm looking for a really good show dog. Can I get one you don't want any more? My ex-husband's five years behind on the child-support payments and I think I'm going to have to move pretty

16

soon and I can come to see your dogs this weekend if I can get out of a meeting I'm supposed to go to with my son's parole officer, gee we can hardly wait to get this show dog and start going to them dog shows and winning all them ribbons and like that.''

Do you think any of these people would get a good show dog (or any dog) from me? Not on your grandmother's shinbone!

A more subtle way of offending a breeder is to assume you are doing him a favor by taking the dog off his hands, or by trying to bargain the price down a notch, which amounts to the same thing. Buying and selling is of course mutually advantageous, both parties need each other. But a successful show breeder with a good reputation for honesty is probably in a position to pick and choose among several prospective buyers. You need him more than he needs you, and you'd be well advised to keep a note of respect in your voice while you get acquainted.

Logistics

As you talk to breeders you'll find some you like and some you distrust instinctively. You're probably wise to follow your instincts. A hard sell in dogs is just as suspicious as a hard sell on the old used car lot. If he's so anxious to trade his dog for your money . . .

Another point to ponder while searching for a breeder is geography. There are advantages and disadvantages to buying close to home. If you've fallen in love with a rare breed you may have no choice in the matter; there may be no breeders in your neck of the woods, or none you feel good about. With the more numerically popular breeds, though, you have wider choices.

Buying close to home means, obviously, less traveling to look at puppies and to learn what you need to learn from the breeder about grooming, training and the dog show ''ropes'' in general. It may also mean getting a dog of lesser quality since you would later be showing at the same shows as the breeder. He knows his dogs, so he's not likely to sell you a better dog than the one he keeps for himself. He may of course guess wrong as to which puppy is the future star, but chances are he knows a whole lot more about how those heads are going to develop, which rears will straighten out with maturity and which will always be bad, than you are likely to know. Some show breeders, unfortunately, love to sell mediocre-quality dogs to new show buyers in their area, because those novices can be counted on to provide easy point-wins for Old Pro.

Buying far afield has its pitfalls. Unless you can get away to do some cross-country window-shopping, you will probably have to trust the breeder and buy sight unseen. This isn't automatically bad, since you wouldn't have the necessary expertise to select a show prospect yourself anyway. If the breeder has wins to back up his claims of quality, and if he seems respected by others in the breed with whom you've spoken, you're probably as safe in buying from this distant source as from a nearby one. In addition, you may just walk into a lucky situation. For instance, a breeder from an opposite coast is eager to place good show stock in homes in other parts of the country to get his stock seen there, and in order not to have to compete against it himself. Sometimes breeders do have more good ones at once than they can use themselves, and it's a benefit to the breeder to get the promising youngsters scattered geographically. Sometimes, too, there are old feuds between the distant breeder and someone in your area, and the breeder will place an extra-good dog with you in hopes you'll cream a rival for him, in absentia. This can work to your advantage, though you'll be starting your show career with a ready-made foe when you turn up in the ring with a dog bred by that rival. So be it. You can survive that, if you got the good dog you wanted.

Why Won't They Sell to Me?

It's a fact of life that the more successful breeders are reluctant to sell their best animals to a total beginner. It may be disheartening for the beginner, but understandable from the breeder's viewpoint. There's nothing more frustrating than being charmed by a charismatic newcomer, selling her a better dog than you really wanted to let go of, spending hours teaching her to groom, giving handling tips and soothing her fears while the pup goes through the adolescent uglies, only to have her and the dog disappear from the scene just as the coat is coming in, the chest is deepening, and the dog is looking like you dreamed he would.

What happened? She decided to go back to school for her

graduate degree and gave the dog to her uncle on the farm because he needed a pet. Or, she found out that dog shows aren't always the garden party she envisioned and decided she wanted no part of them so the dog is neutered and given away. Perhaps she just loves the dog and will always keep him, but her husband says he's not spending his weekends at dog shows and they're not spending any more money on entries. Besides, her kids are starting in Little League now, so they couldn't go to dog shows anyway.

These things happen—a lot. Many breeders who have worked their fannies off to produce just that special head quality, bone structure, and showy movement weep bitter tears when their protégés jump off the bandwagon and drag the superdog with them.

Even if you do stick it out and become a permanent part of the dog show scene, it's probable that you won't do justice to a top dog right away. Top dogs don't happen along very often to begin with. When they do, they are probably the result of expert breeding and anyone astute enough to produce a dog that good is probably wise enough to recognize its quality and hang on to it. If a truly fine dog is born and must be sold, the breeder very probably has friends in the breed who would have first crack at it.

So it's not realistic for a beginner to expect to buy a top show prospect, first try, from a few phone calls.

What you can do, however, is decide on a breeder whom you like and trust, who has proven winners, and then cleave thee only unto him or her until the good show puppy comes along, the one that's right for you. Bear in mind that all successful breeder-exhibitors have enemies. It's a jungle out there, and anyone who breeds and shows regularly, and wins consistently in his area, will generate jealousy and resentment. If you tell Breeder B that you've decided to get a puppy from Breeder A's next litter, you may get an earful of innuendo or worse, aimed at alienating you. B may want to sell you a puppy herself, if only to irritate A; B may want to sell you a puppy herself because she is convinced that hers are wonderful and A's are trash. B may want to chalk up a win over A in this arena because she can't ever get past A in the show ring.

Your best bet is to try to separate truth from fiction, do your homework, make your own judgment calls, then declare your loyalty to the breeder of your choice and stick to it. Don't start making trouble by repeating B's insults; just be cool, but be loyal. You will probably be rewarded, at some point in time, with a very good dog.

Co-ownerships

What about co-ownerships, you ask. Co-ownerships may be suggested by some of the breeders you talk to, and in some cases they can be mutually advantageous. In other instances all the advantage lies with the breeder, so think carefully before you leap at what looks like a good deal.

Some breeders only sell on co-ownerships. They want control over the dog, the show career, and the future breeding. You might for instance be asked to pay what amounts to full price, say $800, for a bitch puppy who must be shown to her championship before she's bred, who must then be bred to a stud of the breeder's selection, and half or more of the litter returned to the breeder, as pure profit. In this way dogs who should never be bred sometimes have litters that should never happen just to pay off co-ownership agreements.

Sometimes a good bitch puppy can be bought at a reduced price, or even be had for nothing, on a co-ownership agreement, and it may be what you want to do. It may also create more problems than you can shake a stud at, and you might live to regret it. What president was it who advised "Avoid entangling alliances"? He probably knew whereof he spoke.

Co-ownerships can be the most direct route to fractured friendships. They are usually designed by the breeder and are usually more to the breeder's advantage than to the buyer's.

My personal philosophy as a breeder is that life's too short for co-ownership hassles, and if the buyer can't afford the initial cost of buying a good dog, he's not likely to show the dog much, travel to where the major wins can be had, stick it out till the championship is completed, or pay for necessary health care. I much prefer an outright sale followed up by as much helpful advice as I can give regarding the dog's show and breeding career. I expect to outlive the rigidly gripping control freaks I see around me, who make their buyers sign contracts about what to feed and how often the dog's nails are to be trimmed.

The Long Way Home

Your best course is to do your homework, and find a breeder to sign on with. Buy an older brood bitch who has produced champions before, who is a champion herself, who is free of genetic problems, and follow the breeder's advice on how to breed her. Raise your own litter of show prospects yourself and select a keeper, again following the breeder's recommendations.

This may seem to be the long way around the bushes, but good older bitches can sometimes be had for a reasonable price, if the breeder likes you and trusts you with her old darling. By raising your own show prospect you get first pick. If there's only one good show prospect in the batch, you get him because you, and only you, are the breeder here. You can keep two or three or eight puppies, grow them out till you know what you have, and then go showing. You'll be starting with stock as good as the original breeder's.

This is good advice but few people have the patience to follow it. I wouldn't, myself, if I were starting over again. I'd buy the first good-looking puppy I held up to my face and fell in love with. That's bad advice, but it's sad reality.

Most books at this point tell you to select your puppy with an eye to signs of good health like pink gums, clear eyes, good flesh, no sign of worms, and no slinking cowardice. Those factors are basic, and would be important in shopping for a pet.

Buying a show dog means looking at slightly different things. By all means check gums and eyes, but if you've selected an ethical, dependable, successful show breeder, the puppies are very probably vaccinated, wormed, and fed. You'll be looking for fine points of conformation in selecting a show prospect, and as a beginner you really won't know enough to make intelligent choices at that level. Experienced breeders are frequently humbled by bad guesses. So the real choice, the important choice is whom to buy from. If you've chosen a good breeder, and if you've been honest with him about what you want and what you intend to do with the dog regarding showing and breeding, you should be able to leave the selection of the puppy itself in the more experienced hands of the breeder.

Registration

Papers. What documents are you entitled to when you buy a pure-bred dog? First and most important, the registration certificate or blue slip. If the dog has already been individually registered with AKC and given its official name, you will get from the breeder a white certificate of registration that will be signed over to you by the breeder when the dog is paid for. If it's to be a co-ownership, then you and the breeder will both be listed as owners. You will then send the signed certificate, along with a small fee, to AKC, and in a month or so a new certificate reflecting the dog's new ownership will be mailed back to you.

If the dog has not yet been individually registered, you will be given a "blue slip," or registration application, signed over to you as the new owner. You will choose a name, fill out the blue slip and send it to AKC with a small fee, and in a month or so AKC will send to you the dog's registration certificate showing you as the new owner.

The breeder will usually have a kennel prefix, one or two words that traditionally are a part of the official name of every dog bred by that person. Be clear with your breeder about that, and go along with his wishes when you name your dog. Some buyers, either through ignorance or design, fail to use the breeder's prefix and instead insert their own brand-new kennel name. If you pull this trick, you doom a valuable relationship.

If you want to start your own kennel name right away, it is acceptable to combine the breeder's and yours, but it's best to clear this with the breeder first. The name might then be Pinecreek's Pretentious of Nottingham, satisfying both the breeder (Pinecreek) and you (Nottingham).

You may notice along the left edge of the blue slip a space for the signature of the owner of the kennel name granting permission for someone else to use it. Ignore it. This pertains only to registered kennel names, and very few breeders still use registered kennel names. This is a holdover from the days of huge, well-financed kennels whose famous prefixes were sometimes pirated by other breeders. The registering of the kennel name with AKC, acted as a sort of copyright protection. These days the pirating is more likely to go the other way, with people who did not breed the dog applying their own kennel names in order to take the bows for future wins. Registering a kennel prefix is expensive and involved, so very few people do, anymore. You are free to make up and use any kennel prefix you want, so long as it doesn't duplicate someone else's.

The Pedigree

The next important document is the pedigree, usually showing four or five generations. This is a family-tree–type listing of parents and grandparents and so on, and although the pedigree may be telling, it may not tell much. If it shows a high percentage of champions, that's good. If most are in the third to fifth generation, whereas the parents and grandparents of your puppy are not champions, that's not so good.

Some pedigrees give other information as well, such as the color of the dogs listed, and that can be helpful, especially if you plan to breed.

One point to remember in reading pedigrees is that in some breeds champions are much more numerous, and titles are much easier to acquire, than in other breeds. In a rare breed there is usually a much higher ratio of champions to registered dogs than in the more populous breeds. "Champion" in a rare breed may simply mean that the breeder built her own points and majors (we'll talk about that later) and finished a lot of her dogs to their championships without ever competing against quality animals. Lots of champions can make for an impressive-looking pedigree, but may not necessarily be quality dogs.

On the other hand, in many breeds a great number of very good dogs never complete championships. Collies, for example, must be shown in full coat or they look awful. It takes a long time to grow a full coat, and the fates frequently decree that just as the big specialty shows with major entries are approaching, the beautiful bitch who just needs that last major to finish her championship, begins shedding huge amounts of coat and by show weekend she looks like anything but a show dog. Then, too, in breeds where professional handlers are dominant in the show ring, owner-handled dogs, no matter how lovely, may never quite get the lucky breaks when they need them.

So when you look at pedigrees, bear in mind whether this is an easy breed to finish, or a hard one, and regulate your impressions accordingly.

Remember, too, the pedigree isn't an official document and it's only as reliable as the breeder is honest and accurate. Even the most reputable breeders can make mistakes in pedigrees; titles added or dropped and names misspelled are typical examples. A lot of copying and typing and margin for error have gone into five generations of pedigree-reproduction.

Other Documents

A health record showing dates of wormings and vaccinations, specifics of what the vaccines cover, and all other relevant data should come with the puppy. Most breeders do their own vaccinations and wormings for the sake of economy. However your puppy was vaccinated, your own vet needs to see the health record to know what has been done.

If you're buying on a co-ownership, then by all means get an agreement in writing that spells out all exigencies. This is your best protection against later misunderstandings and hard feelings. Read it, understand it, and discuss it if necessary before you sign.

Some breeders may supply other papers, too—guarantees, grooming instructions and proof of the sire and dam having been tested for genetic problems are all examples. Ask about them.

Ball Park Numbers

What should you expect to pay for a potential show dog? It varies from breed to breed, and obviously from breeder to breeder and dog to dog, but as you do your research you'll probably find a general price range typical for the breed of your interest. Dogs of rare breeds can cost more than more popular ones. Supply and demand also plays a part. Some breeds cost more to produce than others; some are built so that normal birth is almost impossible and puppies must usually be delivered via Caesarean section. Some breeds require cropped ears. Some have tiny litters. But if you insist on a price quote here, a ''ball park'' figure at the time of this writing for a good young show hopeful will probably range between $500 and $1,000 in most breeds. It's a bargain compared to horses, but expensive compared to baseball cards.

Some breeders have unrealistic opinions of their stock, and ask inflated prices to match. Others may be too timid to ask substantial prices. In the end the old rule of thumb is pretty reliable here—you get what you pay for.

A group of friends from the same kennel club get together for a little informal puppy socializing, invaluable practice for future show dogs.

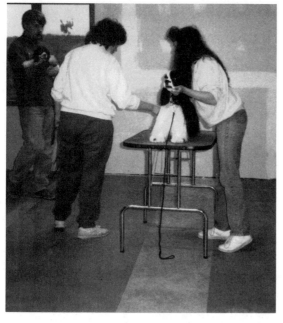

Club members take turns playing judge, to reassure a doubtful young Cocker.

3

Clubs and Matches

NOW YOU HAVE your new show puppy. You're thrilled, you're excited, you're confused on some points and a little scared of what lies ahead. What comes next? How do you jump in and get started?

Most people get into showing by way of the local kennel club. Normally, this is a group of enthusiastic people who show dogs as a hobby. Local kennel clubs operate under AKC rules, and their main activity is the hosting of one or two AKC dog shows each year, always on the same weekends. Because this is a job of mammoth proportions, it takes up most of the club's meeting time and human resources.

In addition to mounting shows, the club will host at least one match a year, matches being small, informal practice shows. It may also conduct a variety of other programs, manage a therapy dog program for taking dogs on nursing home visits, hold Canine Good Citizen tests, host walkathons with dogs, for worthy causes, arrange for speakers to visit schools to give talks on pet care, and more. The American Kennel Club encourages clubs to contribute to their communities, and most members enjoy involvement in one or more of the nonshow activities.

Training Classes

Clubs also hold training classes, usually once or twice a year for eight weeks or so. Depending on the size of the club these may be combinations of obedience and conformation classes, or they may be separate groups on different nights.

Obedience classes are usually divided into beginner and advanced levels, and are open to the public. Beginners learn basic control, heeling on a loose lead, and responding to sit down and come on command. More advanced trainers, usually club members aiming at competing in obedience trials, hone their off-lead heeling, jumping and retrieving, and out-of-sight sits and stays.

These classes are jeans-and-sweatshirt affairs, usually fun, and always social occasions where gossip and show news is traded and friends' dogs are complimented for their improved heeling or quickened recalls. Classes are held in places like school gyms, VFW halls or Army Reserve buildings, and they involve a fair amount of physical labor for a few people, rolling and unrolling and hauling heavy rubber mats that form the floors of the training rings. New members who quietly pitch in and help with this chore are welcomed with gratitude and blessings.

Conformation classes are for preparing new exhibitors and new puppies for careers in the show ring, and that's what you'll be looking for. The word, incidentally, is conFORmation, not conFIRmation as it is so often misspelled even by people who ought to know better. It refers to judging based on the dog's conforming to the standard for its breed. Confirmation, is when the judge agrees with you by making your dog a winner, thereby confirming your opinion.

Conformation classes may be held in conjunction with the club's obedience-class nights, or they may be held at a different time of the year. Often they are scheduled just before the club's annual show, so that members' dogs can be prepared. These class nights, too, are casual affairs as valuable for their camaraderie as for the actual training.

Classes may be structured, with lesson plans and rigid practice routines, or they may be, and generally are, informal workouts with a dozen or so dogs and handlers gaiting around the rubber-matted ring, posing their dogs for the instructor's inspection, and doing individual gaiting patterns in "els" and triangles. The instructor will tell you to get your lead up higher under your dog's throat, keep his head up off the floor, move his hind legs back farther when you stack him and similar tips. Suggestions are usually helpful and the classes are invaluable for getting your puppy accustomed to gaiting on a show lead, being nose to tail with strange dogs, and having strange hands checking his mouth and handling his testicles.

Instructors

The instructor is usually a club member drafted into service, and it may or may not be a person who knows as much as he or she appears to know. Sometime the people who enjoy teaching beginners can be somewhat officious types with egos that feed on the aura of instructorhood. Most are pleasant and helpful, but there is often a tendency toward advising beyond the limit of their knowledge. An instructor who knows nothing about your breed may tell you, for instance, that your dog cannot be shown because it doesn't have a scissors bite, when in fact the correct bite for your breed is an underbite. Puppy buyers have called me in a panic after their first night at training class because the instructor told them their dogs had bad faults, when in fact the instructor had never seen a Bedlington Terrier up close, knew nothing about the standard, and was faulting the dogs for perfectly correct physical features.

Beginners always assume that everyone around them knows everything about dogs and dog shows, because they themselves feel so completely at sea. Wrong, wrong. In some cases the instructor may be the club president, or a "professional handler," or something equally impressive sounding, which may mean nothing more than that they've been at it a while and know some things you don't. But they won't know everything. Usually the fine points of breeds beyond their own are also beyond their frame of reference.

The "New Kid on the Block"

When a brand-new exhibitor with her first dog joins a kennel club, she wears a large scarlet; letter (*N* for Novice) on her breast that is visible to everyone but her. It's only human to want to feel important, and the other club members will revel for a while in having a fresh audience for displays of their wisdom. You will be that audience and they will love you for it, temporarily. It's a recognized fact of dog club life that those who know the least are the most eager to impart their incomplete expertise to the new kid on the block who can be counted on to know even less. It's a high for them. It strokes their egos. But it's not always very dependable advice.

Usually those who know the most sit by watching the blabbermouth advice-spouters, and smiling a little private smile.

The key to happiness here, then, is to politely listen to everyone's outpouring of advice, consider it all, and don't panic over comments about your dog's faults. Gradually the chaff will separate from the grain and you'll find yourself learning what you need to know.

Joining a Club

Most kennel clubs have some sort of application procedure for membership. You may have to be recommended by an existing member or members. You may have to sign a statement promising that you will not wholesale puppies to pet shops, but generally kennel clubs are eager for new members and welcome them warmly. If you don't know anyone in the club, most clubs will welcome you anyway, or invite you to come as a guest for a few meetings. My experience with kennel clubs suggests that big-city clubs tend to be more selective than clubs in small cities and rural areas. These smaller clubs are usually hungry for new recruits in order to keep their membership up to AKC specifications, and to share the workload.

On joining your new club, you may begin to perceive that you are being wooed. Kennel clubs have their subgroups and cliques, clusters of friends and electrically charged poles of animosity. Old grudges left over from the last match when Tina was supposed to stay and help with the cleanup but didn't, and Pete didn't collect for trophy donations like he said he would, so long-suffering Pat had to do it all again like she did every year. A new member can sometimes seem a sort of trophy, to be won away from a rival faction, or a new friend to add to this group or that group.

Here comes some more good advice you won't take. Stay cool and friendly to one and all, but out of entangling alliances, again, until you have time to get acquainted with the whole bunch and follow your own instincts toward friendships. We all tend to be a little uneasy about entering a group of strangers, and the natural thing to do is to hang out with whomever first offers welcome and an interest in your breed. This may be the very person who will indeed become your close friend, but the more widely acquainted you can become before declaring allegiance to one faction or another, the better off you're likely to be in the end.

How do you find a kennel club? The fastest and easiest way is generally to ask at local veterinary hospitals and grooming shops. Kennel clubs don't usually have their own buildings or any sort of permanent phone number, but if there is a club in your area some groomer or veterinary assistant is bound to be a member or know someone who is. A phone call to that member should get you an invitation to come as a visitor to the next club meeting or training class.

Large cities usually have one major club and a scattering of smaller clubs in suburban or outlying areas. Small cities may or may not have a kennel club, but most do. If you live in a rural area, you may be fifty miles or more from the nearest club. At first it may seem too far to commute, but a great number of dog people do just that and consider it a normal way of life. Getting started in showing dogs is much easier, and much more fun, with the help and support of a group of like-minded friends, and kennel clubs are where that group is to be found.

Matches

One major advantage to club membership is that you will have access to information about matches, and matches are the very best way for you and your dog to prepare for dog shows. Every kennel club holds at least one match a year, generally advertising them via flyers sent to other clubs. There are several kinds of matches, which I shall now describe.

Fun matches are very small and informal and are outside the control of AKC. Newly formed kennel clubs that have not yet achieved AKC sanction hold fun matches, and sometimes other clubs do, too, just for experience or to make money for the club. At fun matches the minimum age for the puppy is three months, or sometimes even two months, as opposed to six months for regular dog shows. You needn't enter ahead of time. Your puppy needn't know very much about how to act, and you may be a total, absolute newcomer, without feeling out of place at a fun match. Just throw yourself on the mercy of the judge and the people around you, and you'll find yourself helped, directed and encouraged.

Fun matches usually have only four or five rings. They may or may not include both conformation and obedience judging, and the judges are anyone the club can get to help out. Some are people who want to learn judging in order to go into it seriously, others are judging because they couldn't say no.

In a fun match you may have the only dog of your breed. You'll go through the process of being judged, gaiting your puppy around the ring and posing it for the judge's examination. Usually the judges are good-natured and helpful and can tell you if you're doing something glaringly wrong, or if your dog is obviously not show quality.

After all the breeds in your Group have been judged, assuming you won Best of Breed even if by default, you'll go back in to compete for Best in Group. Group winners then compete for Best in Match. Sometimes the competition is divided between puppies and adults, so that there are separate puppy and adult Bests of Breed, Bests in Group, and Bests in Match.

One notch up from fun matches are Sanctioned B matches. These are very similar to fun matches but are conducted under AKC rules. Most offer puppy classes divided into ages three to six months, six to nine months, and nine to twelve months, and then adult classes, usually just Open Dog and Open Bitch. Puppy classes are also divided by sex.

Above B matches are, of course, Sanctioned A matches. A-level matches are fewer, because they are held only by new clubs

32

At an evening fun match, a young Collie and her handler get a last-minute pep talk from "Grandpa."

Belonging to a kennel club means pulling your share of the load on show day. Ring stewards in obedience trials are frequently called upon to rearrange the patterns of the floor mats to the judge's wishes.

that have held a number of successful B matches and are now working toward AKC permission to host dog shows. A-level matches are considered the club's test of its ability to manage the complexities of a full-scale dog show, so the A match is constructed more like a dog show than a match. Entries must be mailed in advance, the club must publish a judging schedule and catalog, and the classes are basically the same as they would be at a regular show. They start at six months of age and include a full range of classes for adults. Puppies and adults do not have separate Group and Best in Match competitions.

One big difference between matches and shows is that match judges can be anyone in good standing with AKC willing to serve in that capacity, whereas show judges must demonstrate their expertise to be approved by AKC. Part of AKC judging requirements oblige an aspiring judge to officiate at a certain number of matches before he can apply for judging approval. Most match judges are sincerely trying to find the best dog in the ring and put him up, if only to hone their own judging skills. Match judging tends to be free from politics, too, because no one really wants match judging assignments badly enough to exchange wins or favors in order to get them.

While match judging therefore is usually honest, it is of spotty quality from the standpoint of knowledge of the fine points of individual breeds. Some match judges have looked at my dog and said, "Oh, *that's* a Bedlington Terrier." Most people who judge matches are knowledgeable about their own breeds, possibly their own Groups, but few have a trained eye for all of the breeds they may be asked to judge at the match. So it's best to consider the matches as fun and practice, but not to take wins or losses too seriously.

The other big difference between matches and shows is that matches offer no championship points. We'll get into the point system later.

One other difference exists between matches and shows. Matches are for private owners only, no professional handlers are allowed unless they are showing their own dogs. This keeps things fun and reasonably fair, and lowers the level of killer competitiveness.

As your show puppy has been growing up, then, you've been

going to club meetings and training classes, garnering advice good and bad, absorbing opinions about your dog's chances in the show ring, good and bad opinions, and gearing up your skills and your self-confidence toward the big leap into your first real dog show.

But lots of things still confuse you. You're ashamed to admit that you still don't understand about championship points, or what Reserve is. Hang in there, we'll make an expert out of you yet.

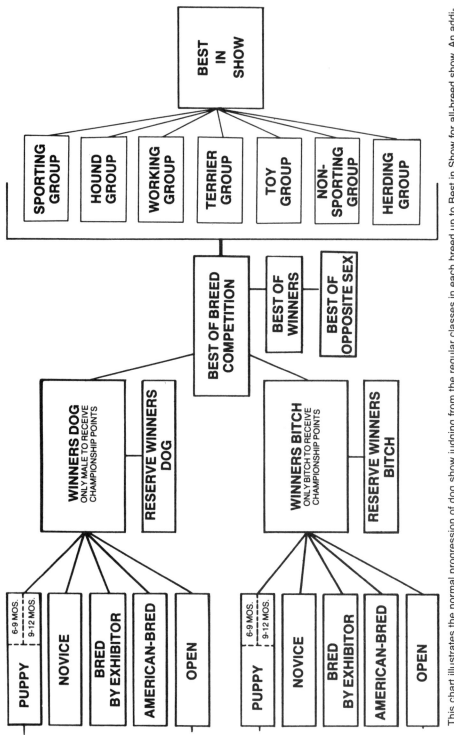

This chart illustrates the normal progression of dog show judging from the regular classes in each breed up to Best in Show for all-breed show. An additional class not shown on this chart is offered at many shows for dogs over twelve but under eighteen months of age. Judging is actually an elimination contest with the Best in Show winner being the only undefeated dog at the end of the show.

From The Complete Dog Book, *18th Edition, 1992, Courtesy of the American Kennel Club*

4

The Progression
of Classes

$\mathbf{A}$ DOG SHOW is a giant process of elimination, beginning with maybe two thousand dogs and ending the day with one supreme winner—always someone else's dog.

Judging goes on all day, simultaneously, in maybe ten or twenty rings, one judge to a ring. Within a breed, the judging will be divided into several classes for males, then several classes for females, then finally the Best of Breed class, for male and female champions plus the top winning male and female nonchampion.

A quick word here about champions. If you're coming into dogs from a background in showing horses or other livestock, dog show championships may be a little confusing, because it is a permanent title, achieved by accumulating points, rather than a "champion of the show" one-time accolade. We'll get into the point system in the next chapter; for now, just remember that show dogs are either champions or nonchampions, better known as "class" dogs and "class" bitches.

Regular Class Judging

Males and females are shown in separate classes in order to give females a fair shot at the championship points. In many breeds the males are simply more impressive looking than the females—bigger, bolder, fuller-coated. Bitches in coated breeds tend to shed, or blow, their coats when they are in season, putting them at a disadvantage in the show ring. Hence, separate classes for males, which are generally termed ''dogs,'' and for females, termed ''bitches.''

You will know that you've graduated from the novice ranks when you can talk about bitches without feeling uncomfortable.

A breed is judged in its entirety, all at once, all in the same ring, and all under the same judge. It will begin with Puppy Dogs, proceed through all the Dog classes, then Winners Dog; it will then recommence with Puppy Bitch, proceed through all the bitch classes, then Winners Bitch, and climax with the Best of Breed class.

I'll go into the various classes in more detail in a minute; this is just to give you an overview.

When each of the dog classes has been judged, then the first in each of those classes all come back into the ring to compete for Winners Dog. This is the breath-holder, the heart-stopper, because this is where the precious championship points are awarded, and for most exhibitors, winning the championship, or ''finishing'' the dog, is the goal of the game.

Winners Classes

The Winners class is judged and one dog receives the coveted plum—Winners Dog!

After that comes the designation of Reserve Winners Dog, and this is where it can get confusing if you haven't yet grasped the concept. The function of the Reserve is to have a next-in-line winner standing literally in reserve, in case, for some reason, the Winners Dog should later be declared ineligible. This happens rarely, but it is possible that the dog might be found to have been entered illegally or was for some reason ineligible to compete. If, for instance, the dog's owner or co-owner was under suspension from AKC privileges at the time of the show, any dog owned by that person would be ineligible to compete. A competitor might complain to the show committee that the winning dog was faked in some way, surgically or otherwise. If at a later hearing the allegations are found to be correct, the dog's points would be taken from him.

If Winners points must be taken away from the dog designated Winner at the show, the points then are awarded to the Reserve Winner.

Reserve, then, goes to the next-best in the Winners class. The judging is between the remaining first-place winners, after the selection of Winners Dog, but with one addition. The dog who placed second to the Winners Dog in its original class is also eligible to compete. If Winners Dog came from the Open class, then the dog who was second in Open is eligible to compete for Reserve, and he comes back into the ring immediately after the selection of Winners Dog.

For example, suppose there are entries in Puppy, American-bred, and Open dogs. These three classes are judged. The three winners come back into the ring for Winners Dog. The judge selects the Open dog as her Winners. The Puppy and American Bred remain in the ring, and the dog who placed second in the Open class nips back into the ring. The judge will probably just take a quick look at that dog before deciding on Reserve, which might be any before her.

This may seem an unnecessarily cumbersome procedure, but its goal is fairness. Imagine how you'd feel if your dog came in second in a big, tough class to a dog who had no legal right to be shown there. Suppose that dog won a major point win in the Winners class, points that would have completed your dog's championship. If the dog who defeated yours for the points was disqualified for some infraction, you'd feel cheated yourself, out of the fair chance your dog should have had, at those points. The Reserve system provides that chance.

Back to our theoretical show—all of the dog classes have now been judged, and all but one of the class dogs have been eliminated from further competition. Only the Winners Dog remains in the game. Judging recommences then with the bitch classes, Puppy through Open, then Winners and Reserve. Everyone but the Winners Bitch is eliminated.

Best of Breed Class

Then and only then do dogs who already have their championships come into the game. This means that nonchampions don't have to compete for points with finished champions, as they do in many European countries.

Into the ring they come, in traditional order—male champions, female champions, Winners Dog, Winners Bitch. All are judged, though the judge probably won't examine the Winners Dog and Winners Bitch as closely as the others, having just seen them.

There are three designations to be made now; Best of Breed, Best of Winners, and Best of Opposite Sex to Best of Breed. Best of Breed might be any of the champions (call them specials if you want to sound like a pro), or it could be either Winners Dog or Winners Bitch. It's all up to the judge.

If the judge selects one of the male specials as Best of Breed, then he will choose a Best Opposite, which will be either a bitch special or Winners Bitch.

If Best of Breed is a bitch, then Best Opposite will be one of the male specials or Winners Dog.

Best of Winners will be selected following Best of Breed and prior to judging for Best of Opposite Sex, and this can be another breath-holder for the exhibitors, because it can make a big difference in the points awarded. Best of Winners is selected between just two, the Winners Dog and the Winners Bitch. Best of Winners receives the maximum number of points awarded that day in that breed. Points will be explained later; suffice it to say that some dogs finish their entire championships on Best of Winners points, so this designation is frequently more important than Winners Dog or even Best of Breed.

Of the three final designations, some can be doubled up. That is, Best of Breed and Best of Winners may be the same dog, or Best of Opposite and Best of Winners. For instance, if there are no bitch specials entered, then Best of Opposite automatically goes to Winners Bitch, who might also be decreed Best of Winners.

Group and Best in Show Judging

Now, let's proceed to the next level of the process of elimination. All day the breed judging has been progressing in all those rings, and finally, around midafternoon, breed judging concludes, leaving just one survivor in each breed—the Best of Breed winner. These dogs will then compete for Best in Group.

All breeds fall into seven Groups—Sporting, Hound, Working, Terrier, Toy, Non-Sporting and Herding. I've listed them in what is termed "catalog order," but they may be judged in whatever order best suits the schedule, whichever Group has concluded breed-level judging first.

Group judging is pretty simple. The breed winners for the Sporting Group, for instance, come into the ring, probably some twenty eligibles. Some breeds won't be represented because there were no entries at that show, or because the owner of the breed winner chose not to compete in the Group. It's not mandatory. The judge selects his placements, first through fourth, and may also do a "cut," or pull-out, in which he selects maybe eight or nine favorites, dismisses the rest of the Group, then makes a final selection from among the survivors. This is a way in which judges can designate to exhibitors and ringside spectators which dogs he really likes, even though there aren't enough placements to go around. Bragging about making the cut in a tough Group can be almost as much fun as bragging about a Group placement.

When all the Groups have been judged, the Group winners come back into the ring to go for the "big enchilada," Best In Show. There is only one placement here, no second, third, or fourth places, no Best of Opposite. It's all or nothing and a moment of high excitement.

Best, as the insiders casually refer to it, is everyone's dream, but the Bests almost always go to top show dogs presented by well-known professional handlers. It's wise not to hang your heart on that dream, but it's fun to try. Most owner-handlers show dogs all their lives without ever winning a Best, and most have no expectation of doing so. Secret dreams maybe . . .

INSIDER'S GUIDE TO THE REGULAR CLASSES

Let's go back for a minute and look at the classes, because you'll have to decide which class to enter your dog in when you start showing.

It's legal to enter more than one class, but almost no one ever does, for a very good reason. In order to qualify for the Winners class you'd have to win every class you entered, so why risk your shot at the points by entering two classes and having to win both, when winning just one would qualify you for the all-important Winners round? Back in the early years of dog shows it was the custom to offer cash prizes, or "premiums," so in those days people entered as many classes as they qualified for, in hopes of cashing in. As a leftover from that time, the entry information pamphlet for a show is still called a premium list.

But you're not going to make the beginners' mistake of entering more than one class. I raised you better than that! You'll decide which class is best for your dog, not always an easy guess, by the way. Here are the classes you have to choose from:

PUPPY: In breeds with large entries there are usually two puppy classes offered, split by age. Puppy Dog 6 to 9 Months, and Puppy Dog 9 to 12 Months. If your puppy is over nine months old on the day of the show, he goes into Nine to Twelve. The 6 to 9 class covers dogs who are over six months old but not yet nine months old on the date of the show.

There are advantages and disadvantages to entering in Puppy class. If your dog looks obviously immature, narrow, gangly, coatless, or shallow-bodied or if his ring behavior still needs work, judges will probably be more forgiving if he is in the Puppy class. On the other hand, some judges make a policy of never giving Winners points to puppies on the theory that a beautiful puppy will not necessarily mature into a good dog, or even a showable dog. These judges don't want to appear foolish for having given early points to a dog who turns out to be a disaster. So if your puppy looks good, looks pretty much like an adult dog, and is confident and well behaved, you may be in a better position to win points if you enter him in Open.

Although some judges are reluctant to put up puppies, other judges seem to have a weakness for puppy-cuteness or for being the first to find and promote a hot youngster. Whether or not to show in Puppy classes can depend just as much on who is judging as on how your puppy looks. This is information you probably won't have until you've been showing for a while and have started learning about judges, but you can ask around, before you fill out your entry, and see if anyone at your kennel club meeting or training class knows that judge's feelings about putting up puppies.

TWELVE TO EIGHTEEN: The 12-to-18 Month class is for dogs twelve to eighteen months of age. You probably didn't need me to tell you that. It's a very handy class because many breeds mature slowly, and a dog that is too old for regular puppy classes may still be shallow, narrow, undeveloped and unready to go head-on with fully mature adults. This class, like the American-Bred and Bred-by Exhibitor class, can be useful if your breed draws big numbers with huge entries in the Open classes, and little chance for being noticed among more experienced handlers—amateur and professional.

NOVICE: The Novice class is for any dog that has not yet won a championship point, a first place in any other adult class, or three firsts in Novice classes. You may feel drawn to this class because it sounds safe and nonthreatening, but don't enter it. Although judges may have an indulgent or sympathetic bent toward exhibitors in this class, they almost never take them seriously in Winners, where it counts. By entering Novice you are telling the world that you are brand-new at this, you have no faith in yourself, and you have no faith in your dog whether you do or you don't.

I was once watching Collie judging at a small midwestern show, when a man came into the ring in the Novice class, so frightened that all the ringside watchers whimpered under our breaths in sympathy for him. He was the only entry. He tripped over his dog, stood in the wrong place, dropped his lead and fell through the ring fencing. The poor man was miserable. The judge humanely kept his examination brief, patted the man's arm a lot, and told him to take first place.

The man stumbled gratefully to the wooden place marker on the floor bearing the number One, picked it up, and bolted from the ring. The steward, once she had caught her breath, went running after him waving and screaming, and towed him back to the ring to receive his ribbon. No one wanted to laugh at the poor man, but it was impossible to hold it in. Judging continued and the man's dog was eventually given Reserve, very possibly a sympathy gesture on the judge's part.

Remember this story when you make your first embarrassing goof in public at a dog show. You are not alone.

You may be a novice, you may feel like one, but try not to broadcast the fact by entering the Novice class.

BRED-BY-EXHIBITOR: This class is for dogs that were bred, that are owned, and that are actually taken into the ring, all by the same person. Assuming you're starting your show career with a puppy bought from someone else because you didn't take my good advice about starting with a proven brood bitch, this class won't be an option for you. Later, when you are showing a dog you bred yourself, you may want to use this class, or you may not. It's a good class for people who are proud to have bred the dog they're showing. But judges' prejudices must be considered here, too, and there are judges who look with less favor, in their Winners classes, on all entries except the Open class winner.

The number of dogs being shown can be important here. If yours is a popular breed in which the Open classes may have twenty or thirty entries, you may have a better chance of being seen, and really looked at, if you enter one of the smaller classes.

AMERICAN-BRED: This one is a holdover from earlier decades when many show dogs were imported from other countries, and the AKC wanted to promote the breeding and showing of dogs in this country. Currently it's used for dogs with little chance of winning. A dog considered by its owner to be unable to win in Open might be entered in American-Bred, but in the circumstances, one wonders why the dog was entered at all. It might have been entered as a "filler," an extra dog whose purpose it is to make points for another, better, dog usually, but not always, owned by the same exhibitor. This is often done in rare breeds, where perhaps only one person in the area exhibits dogs of that breed. Without a filler dog to make points, there would be no competition, and therefore no points. If the owner wanted to handle all her entries herself, she might put fillers in puppy, American-Bred, and Bred-By, plus the best dog in Open.

I personally don't believe its a good idea to enter in American-Bred. Like the Novice class, it announces to the world that you believe your dog can't win in Open.

OPEN: This is the serious class, where the best of the class dogs and bitches are likely to be entered. Open is, as the name implies, open to just about any dog that can be shown. Puppies over six months can enter, dogs bred in any country whose stud book is recognized by AKC can enter, and in fact finished champions can enter. This is sometimes done to add fillers, to make points, if a rare breed exhibitor needs to bring four dogs, in order to make a major (we'll talk about majors later) for instance, and doesn't have enough young dogs. She might enter a retired champion in Open just to build points. This practice, however, is not encouraged.

More Winners Dogs and Winners Bitches come out of the Open class than all other classes combined, with Puppy classes in second place and Bred-By in third. If you are serious about going for the points and the championship, and if your dog looks mature and acts reasonably well, Open is probably your best bet. Although it's easier to win the smaller classes, Bred-By and American-Bred, thus getting into the Winners class more easily, you still have to get past the Open winner in order to get the points. This is a matter of individual strategy, and some people would argue this point with me. Many have, in fact.

You'll need to work out your own strategy.

Here comes another bit of excellent advice that you probably won't take—at least in the beginning. I seldom have the self-control to take it myself, but I'm convinced that it is the best bit of wisdom I've picked up from listening to successful old-timers. It is this: Wait till your dog looks like a champion. Then start to show him.

If you do that, you will come into the ring with built-in advantages over the other beginners, and many of us old hands who should know better, who jump into the ring too soon, with immature youngsters whose bodies haven't yet filled out and muscled up, whose coats are not the length or texture they should be, and who still act tentatively about crowds and judges.

Starting dogs before they are ready is one of the most common beginner mistakes, a mistake that is shared by a great number of old-timers, this author included.

Our excuse for showing prematurely is that the dogs need ring experience, but ring experience can be acquired at matches and training classes. The real reason we tend to show our young dogs too soon is that, to us, they look so beautiful, so ready, so superior to the competition, that we can't wait.

Maybe you'll be smarter.

Maybe not.

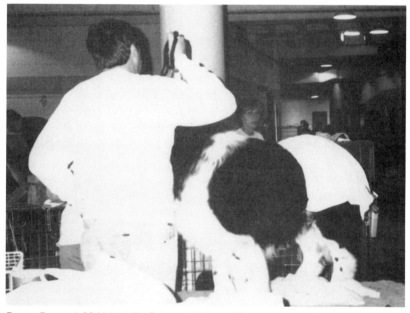

Doggy Depends?? Not really. Some exhibitors will use some version of the arrangement shown when their bitches come in season while they are on show premises.

5

The Point System

CHAMPIONSHIP POINTS are the markers in the game. For the average owner-handler, the goal in showing a dog is to win its championship. This is a permanent title that becomes an official prefix to the dog's name on his registration and on the pedigrees of his offspring. A champion is a star and carries with him the aura of dog-world acclaim. It is a fate devoutly to be sought by the dog's owner because it is a solid achievement that no one can take away, and that others will respect as long as the dog lives.

Finishing a dog, that is, completing his championship, is a high that has to be experienced. The feeling is beyond description, and for many dogfolk, it beats anything else going.

A quick terminology lesson here: finishing means completing a championship title, after which, if the dog continues to be shown, he becomes a "special." Specialing a dog means campaigning him for wins on the higher level, going for Bests of Breed, for Group wins, for Bests in Show if you dream big.

To finish, your dog must win fifteen points, including two or more "major" wins, under at least three different judges.

Points are awarded to two dogs of each breed at each show, to the Winners Dog and to the Winners Bitch, provided there is competition within the sex.

The number of points awarded will be from none to five, depending on the number of dogs in competition, and on the point scale, which I'll talk about in a minute. Wins of one or two points are considered minor wins, and wins of three, four, or five points are major wins, or majors. These are the hotly sought-after and elusive wins that separate the men from the boys, the champions from the near-misses.

There are ways to increase the number of points won: by going Best of Winners, by winning Best of Breed or Best of Opposite Sex, by winning a Group first, or by winning Best in Show. Whoever is designated Best of Winners will receive the same number of points as either Winners Dog or Winners Bitch, whichever is higher.

If your dog wins Best of Breed from the classes, then goes on to win first in the Group (okay, we're dreaming here, but just suppose), he would be awarded as many points as was awarded that day in any breed competing in that Group. And if he goes on to win Best in Show (why wish for a loaf of bread when you can wish for the grocery store) he would get the highest number of points awarded that day, for any breed at that show.

The available points are figured on a basis of actual dogs competing that day. Absentees don't count. Any dog that is disqualified, excused from the ring for limping or any other reason, any dog from whom all awards are withheld, these don't count. And the champions don't count. Only the class dogs or bitches count, and only those who actually compete. "Class" dogs are nonchampions. So if there are nine class dogs entered, including yours, and seven of them actually show up and compete, and your dog takes Winners, he gets whatever number of points an entry of seven males in that breed at any show in that area of the country warrants.

You can determine the operative point scale by contacting AKC, by asking someone who shows in your breed, or by looking it up in the May issue of AKC's *Events Calendar*, in which the newly revised point scales are published each year. Or you can look it up in the show catalog on the day of the show. If you are confused as to how many points you just won, ask at the superintendent's table at the show; they're used to sorting out confused winners.

Points, by the way, are invisible. You aren't handed anything in the ring that designates that you have just won a specific number of points, other than the purple Winners ribbon. The points are magically computed behind the scenes and go directly from the superintendent's records to AKC's records. All point wins are published monthly in the Show Awards Section of *Pure-Bred Dogs— American Kennel Gazette*, and when, according to AKC, your dog has completed his title, AKC will send you a championship certificate.

It will be well worth your while to subscribe to the *Gazette*, checking the *Show Awards* section when you begin showing and winning, because mistakes are made by judges, by superintendents, and by AKC itself. You may have a finished champion according to your records, but no certificate arrives. It might have been your error in figuring your points, or it might have been someone else's error, but if you can go back through your Awards issues covering the shows where you won your points, you can verify your own calculations, or see where the difference lies between your reckoning and AKC's. You may have thought a certain win was a major, but AKC's records show it as only a two-point win. When in doubt, you can call AKC and ask for a verification of your dog's points, and if you disagree, you can present your facts to AKC's Show Records department and hope it will be straightened out. It usually is.

I thought I'd finished a dog a few years ago, but noticed that in the Awards listing, one of his majors was shown as a two-point win. There had been two points for Best of Winners, but he had also gone on to Best of Breed over a special, making it a major and completing his championship. I called AKC to check with its records and we discovered that the judge had written the placement in her official judge's book as Best of Winners, not Best of Breed. I had a photo taken that day, for the Best of Breed win, and I had kept the ribbon. I wrote to the judge, sending her a copy of the win picture and a photocopy of the ribbon. She remembered the show, apologized profusely for her error, and wrote to AKC, which promptly changed the records and sent on the championship certificate.

To help clarify this point business, which can be confusing, let's run through a few for instances: You are showing a male Basenji. He is the only male entered, but there are four bitches entered. Four bitches is worth two points, in that geographical division. Your dog gets no points for Winners Dog because he didn't beat any competition, but he does go Best of Winners, which gives him two points. You're not taking them away from the Winners Bitch; she gets to keep her two points also, so don't feel bad about that.

Suppose you're showing your male Basenji at a show where there are three males, two females, two male specials and one female special. You get lucky and take Best of Breed. In this case you get to add all three of the specials in with the class dog entry, so you'd have three class dogs plus three specials for a total of six "males," for the purpose of figuring how many points you just won.

Now suppose it's the same show and same entry, but Best of Breed goes to the bitch special. You beat the two male specials for Best of Opposite. In this case you get to add the two male specials, but not the bitch special. This would give you a total of five entries to count, in figuring your points—the three class dogs and the two dog specials.

If you won Best of Breed, picking up, say, two points, then went on to win the Hound group, and there had been a four-point major in Afghans that day, your win would become four points instead of two—not in addition to, but instead of, your two breed points. If you went on to win Best in Show (okay, laugh a lot here, this is just so you'll understand the system), and any breed shown that day had a five-point major entry, then your win would become five, rather than four points, but you'd be flying so high by that time, you wouldn't care about the extra point.

Understanding the Point Scale

The point scale is a somewhat elaborate system by which AKC determines the points available in each breed, in each group of states (termed divisions), each year. It is based on the number of dogs of that breed competing in shows in that geographical division during the previous year. This is necessary because entries vary so widely

50

from breed to breed, and from one part of the country to the next. The scale is also divided by sex, with bitches usually needing slightly larger entries to make the same number of points as dogs, because in most breeds, entries are higher in bitches than in dogs.

In a popular breed in which an average entry for a smallish show in the Midwest is forty dogs, the point scale might decree that it takes three bitches to make one point, six bitches to make two points, thirteen bitches to make a three-point major, eighteen bitches to make four points, and twenty-four bitches to make the maximum win, a five-point major. This would mean that some shows might not offer any points at all, an average-sized show might offer two points, and a really big show could yield four or five points.

By the same token, a rare breed having no entries at all in some states and very small entries even at large shows might have a point scale at the lowest end of the range, or "in the basement," in old-pro terminology. In the basement means an entry of two for one point, three for two points, four for a three-point major, five for a four-point major, and six for a five-pointer.

The point system, like the income tax system, may seem complex at first glance but it is based on optimum fairness and once you grasp it, its logic becomes clear. It may seem unfair that some dogs only have to beat three competitors to get a major whereas others may have to beat thirty for the same number of points. But by and large, it is just as hard to find three competitors in a rare breed as to find thirty in a popular one.

AKC has set up a system that is as fair as it is possible to make it; however, the odds are unavoidably going to favor some over others. For one thing, it is much easier to finish a dog of a rare breed than of a popular breed simply because you have better odds of being best out of four than of being best out of thirty. This is especially true if you are a beginner without the skills that get your dog noticed by judges sorting out huge entries.

Also, it is much easier to engineer majors in a rare breed, and this is exactly what many people do. If it only takes four to make a major, its often possible for one or two people in that breed to get together and build a major entry with the addition of fillers, or point-makers. These might be very young puppies, older dogs sold locally as pets, or out-of-condition brood bitches from the kennel. In this way it's quite possible to show a mediocre dog to its championship undefeated, because it's never had to go up against genuine competition. In the end, this does more harm than good.

On the other hand, the more popular the breed, the lower the overall quality can be, so that in an entry of thirty Cocker Spaniels there might be ten good ones and twenty mediocres. An entry of five Clumber Spaniels might well mean five good ones, since Clumbers are usually bred by serious dogfolk, specifically for the ring.

In spite of the rule of thumb that says, the more popular the breed the lower its average quality, it is still a fact that it's easier to finish champions in rare breeds than in popular ones, and the ratios of dogs competing to dogs finishing, in these breeds, bears this out. The exception is breeds so rare that there are no points available in your traveling range at all.

Thus the championship title takes on different values in different breeds. In a medium-rare breed it might be considered a rather minimal proof of quality, something to enjoy but not to worship excessively. In an average-population breed, it is to be respected as a solid achievement. In a high-population breed it is a rare accomplishment, and dogs who haven't achieved it are not necessarily to be scorned. No one will throw rotten fruit at a Sheltie who won twelve points and a major in tough competition, but never quite managed to be in the right place at the right time under the right judge, for that last major.

Allowing for differences in breeds, it is still a pretty fair system. The necessity for two major wins serves as a workable safeguard, in most breeds, against cheap champions, especially since the two majors must come from two different judges, and a third judge must have given at least one of the other points along the way. In other words, at least three judges must have put up your dog, and two of them must have given him major wins, before he can be officially finished. This precludes the possibility of showing an inferior dog until you find one judge who likes him, then following that judge all over the country until he has put up your dog fifteen times.

It's much easier in Canada, for instance. A Canadian championship only requires ten points—no majors. Because Canadian shows are much smaller than American events, it is quite possible to

52

"This is boring. Bring on the cows."

show one clinker against your own point-maker who is even worse, go to a few three-show weekends with no other competition in your breed, and presto, you can have a champion.

If you do win two majors under the same judge, the second one will count as points, but you'll need to keep on truckin' until you win an additional major under someone else. Say your dog has eleven points and one major under Joe Judgely. You show under Mr. Judgely again and win a four-pointer, but you still don't have a champion. You have fifteen points and two majors, but you need an additional major under one more judge.

I recently finished two champions at the same show, a dog and a bitch, and each finished with twenty-four points, rather than fifteen. Each had won a first major early on, and then there had been no majors available in my area for months. I showed anyway, in the hope of picking up a Best of Breed win at shows with class entries worth only two points but with specials that might have made the wins majors, if either dog had won Best of Breed. Worth a shot, right?

In some cases, extra points were won by one or both of the pair because there had been a major entry in bitches; my bitch won Winners and my dog won Best of Winners, which would have finished both, but one bitch was absent, so the bitch major ''broke'' and my dogs accumulated needless minor points to add to their piles.

Although it's considered okay to win more than your required two majors, that is, to hit a lucky streak and win three or four, or even five majors on your way to finishing, it's generally frowned upon to deliberately snarf up minor points you don't need. If your dog already has all his minor points and only needs majors, you might enter at several shows that don't have major entries even with the addition of specials. If you win, you're taking minor points you don't need from someone else who might have needed them. Doing it routinely will lose you friends. If you are trying for a possible Best of Winners or Best of Breed major, that's acceptable and not considered poor sportsmanship.

If you routinely break majors by pulling your dog (not showing him at the last minute), this too will earn you a bad name in the sportsmanship department, especially from the people who stood to win the majors you broke. Majors are precious, and anyone who spoils them for frivolous reasons is asking for animosity.

Sometimes antagonistic competitors will break majors deliberately, by pulling entries. Mary and Jane might hate each other's guts for past insults; maybe Mary didn't want to breed to Jane's stud dog and bred instead to a stud owned by Jane's bitter enemy, Joan. Mary and Jane have now been sniping at one another politely for the last year or so, and are now competing head-on. Mary is campaigning her puppy sired by Joan's dog. It's imperative to Jane that Mary's dog not finish before hers (sired by her own stud, of course) because she has to drive home the point to Mary that she was stupid not to have bred to Jane's superior stud.

So far, Mary's puppy has been beating Jane's more often than not, and a win today would finish him. He needs that last major to finish. There is only one point available in dogs, but there is a major entry in bitches, including Jane's puppy, who is a bitch. Now, Jane wants the major on her bitch, but her bitch is in tall company and isn't likely to win it. Mary's dog, however, has an excellent shot at picking up the Best of Winners points because he's a nice dog, because the judge likes to give away point splits whenever he can (I'll explain point splits in a minute), and because the judge has a track record for putting dogs over bitches for Best of Winners.

If Jane's bitch is pulled from competition, then Mary's dog can't finish that day, because the major will have been broken—no major, no championship, even with the Best of Winners point split.

Jane decides her bitch has a headache and just doesn't feel like showing. A small nasty victory, score one for Jane. Nothing is proven, of course, about the relative quality of the pups or the studs, and Mary knows perfectly well that she's been had.

Building Majors

It's fairly common among exhibitors of less popular breeds to agree ahead of time that everyone in an area will enter at a specific show, with enough entries to make a major in one sex or other, usually in bitches. A three-show weekend is ideal for this, because it gives the opportunity to make majors for perhaps two or three exhibitors. In some breeds, this is the only hope of finding majors. Usually one of the exhibitors who is in on the gambit is likely to get the wins. Judges, however, are hard to predict, and sometimes an outsider walks into a setup weekend and takes home all the cookies. This makes the organizers fume behind their congratulatory smiles, and makes the interlopers laugh a lot while driving home.

As you come onto the scene within your breed and begin to show your dog and get acquainted with your fellow exhibitors, be aware that you may be warmly invited to this show or that show. It may be because they love you. It may be because you, as the newcomer, are considered a source of easy points for more seasoned exhibitors. Newcomers generally do make easy points for others. They frequently have dogs that are less than wonderful and often start showing before their dogs are ready for serious competition, and in a breed that requires skill in grooming, their dogs are likely to be at additional disadvantage.

This explains at least some of the warmth with which new people are welcomed aboard. It is human nature. Accept it impersonally, laugh it off, but don't be a sucker if you can help it. If you don't feel your dog is ready to be a serious contender for the points, don't feel socially obligated to serve as an easily defeatable point-maker for the others.

Splitting Points

You may hear people talk about point-splitting: Judge So and So never splits points, or likes to split points, or someone is going for the point split. Splitting points just means that the Best of Winners goes to whichever animal will most benefit from it. If Winners Dog is worth no points because there was only one entry, but Winners Bitch is worth a three-point major, and if the judge gives Best of Winners to the dog, that's a point split.

Some judges routinely split points, that is, give Best of Winners to whichever of the two Winners will most benefit. It's a fairly painless way to make exhibitors happy, and this may be to the judge's benefit. Some judges routinely do this, no matter what the relative qualities are of the two dogs in contention. This of course is not good judging and AKC rightly frowns on the practice. Unfortunately, it is not possible to legislate human nature.

Some judges appear prone to give Best of Winners to the male, regardless of his quality. Since most breeds have larger entries in bitches than in dogs, this can mean many males picking up many point splits, and often finishing championships much more easily than bitches of the same breed.

In my breed in my area, it is not at all unusual for a male to complete his entire championship on Best of Winners point splits, never having defeated another dog of his sex. It's the same in many rare breeds. Although this makes it fun and easy to finish champions, it also makes the championship title less a measure of an individual dog's quality.

The trick here is to adjust your expectations to the breed of your choice, and play the game realistically. If you're in a popular breed where only a small percentage of dogs being shown ever finish their championships, then owning a champion may not be a realistic goal. Winning classes might be a better target, at least for starters.

If you've chosen a rare breed, and if you live in an area where competition is available and you have a good dog, then a championship might be a realistic goal. In fact, it might be too quickly completed. In that case you may want to consider the idea of specialing your dog. Or you might want to branch out into other areas with him, such as obedience, hunting titles, tracking, agility or flyball teams.

Championships are wonderful, but they aren't the whole game, by any means.

Ranking Systems

There is another kind of point system but it has nothing to do with championships.

Several dog magazines keep tabs on show wins and publish "top ten" rankings monthly, quarterly, or yearly. There might also be top twenty dogs in each Group, or the top hundred dogs of all breeds. These ranking systems change frequently. To try to name publications or systems here would date this book immediately.

Each system is set up slightly differently, and each gives an advantage to a somewhat different segment of the competition. One magazine, for instance, runs two ranking systems and publishes results in every month's issue. It's a great way to sell magazines. One system awards one point for every dog defeated in Best of Breed wins. The other system awards points for every dog defeated in Breed, Group, and Best in Show competition. Other magazines' systems might award points only for Group and Best in Show. Some give one point for each dog defeated, others use sliding scales—one point for one to five dogs defeated, two points for six to ten dogs, and so forth.

In a one-for-one ranking system, with a point for each dog defeated in breed wins, your dog would get nine points for a Best of Breed win at a show in which ten dogs of your breed were entered and actually competed, the tenth being your own dog.

Under this system, if your dog won a Group first in the Working Group at a show at which there was a total of ninety-seven entries present among all the Working breeds, your dog would get ninety-six points.

If your dog won a Group third, you'd get points for the total number of dogs entered in those breeds, minus the number entered in the two breeds represented by the first- and second-place dogs. Confused? Let me run that by you again. You won third place with your Great Pyrenees. Group first was won by a Boxer, and Group second by a Bernese Mountain Dog. In the Working Group at that show there was a total of fifty entries, including four Boxers and two Bernese. Your dog, in third place, would win forty-three points, fifty total entries minus the four Boxers, the two Bernese, and itself. This computes because your dog didn't beat the Boxer or the Bernese who in turn beat the others in their respective breeds. And you didn't beat yourself.

Sometimes a Group fourth might be worth more points than a Group first at another show. It would depend on the total entry in that Group, and it would depend on the number of dogs in the breeds that produced the animals to place above yours. If your dog came in second in a big Group, beaten only by a French bulldog who was the only Frenchie entered, your dog would get points equal to the total Group entry, minus only your dog and the one Frenchie. But if your dog got a Group second behind a Bichon Frise that was in a breed entry of fourteen, your dog would get a lot fewer points.

Generally speaking, the systems that count only Best of Breed wins are more fair than those that count breed, Group, and Best in Show wins, because competition gets progressively more subjective at these levels. Breed level wins tend to reflect more closely the actual quality of the dogs than do Group level wins.

These ranking system points are not official; they are not awarded by AKC, but only by the individual publications. Some titles, however, such as Top Show Dog—All Breeds and Top Dog in each Group, carry quite a bit of prestige, and may include formal awards banquets, big trophies, the works. These wins almost invariably go to dogs owned by those who can afford the financial burden of a serious campaign, so don't eat your heart out over them.

Still, if you are specialing a dog in a rare breed where few dogs are being campaigned, it is within the realm of possibility for your dog to make it into the Top Ten, and that is exciting. You will run off copies of the rating sheet and carry them to work with you, boring friends and strangers alike.

Dog show rigs range from the last word in luxury to the . . . homemade and most modest.

6

Gearing Up: How to Enter, What Stuff to Buy

THE TIME IS ALMOST UPON US. Your show prospect puppy is beginning to look ready, he's behaving reasonably well at training class, and you want to go showing. Okay, so he doesn't look like a champion yet but you've decided to ignore my good advice and jump in anyhow, for the sake of ring experience. That's all right. You'll be making easy points for the other guys for a while but when you're starting out with your very first dog, the excuse of needing ring experience is probably justified.

Everyone is nervous for those first few shows, and it's not entirely wrong to want to get the jitters out of the way while your dog is still less than prime. You can justify this on the theory that by the time you're comfortable about handling in the ring, your dog will have also settled into the routine and will have finished muscling up and growing coat. Then at some point down the road, the two of you will emerge as genuine competition.

The ideal would be to get the ring experience for man and beast at matches rather than point shows, because matches are less expensive to enter and offer more hope of winning. But there may not be that many matches available, and never when you need them. Sometimes we all jump in too soon, at shows instead of matches, just because WE WANT TO.

When you feel almost ready to take the plunge, write or call all the show superintendents who service your area (we'll talk more about them later) and ask to be put on their mailing list for premium lists. It may take more than one phone call in some cases, but you should start receiving premium lists soon after, and these will contain the entry forms and information you'll need.

Meanwhile, check your equipment, and order what you need. There are some excellent kennel supply catalogs available; you can probably borrow a few from kennel club friends until you get on mailing lists yourself. After that there'll be no shortage of catalogs coming at you. Take my word.

Crates

If you don't already have a crate, that should head your shopping list. And don't call them cages, or people will know you're a beginner. Crates. They come in several basic types—the solid ones made of fiberglass or plastic and sometimes referred to as airline crates, and the open-air kind made of wire mesh. Some exhibitors like wood crates while others prefer all-aluminum versions.

Plastic crates are lightweight, easy to clean, and offer the dog privacy, which can be important, especially to a somewhat timid dog. In scary places like dog show buildings the green show dog can curl up in his own familiar private place and feel safe. This is conducive to napping, which can result in a more relaxed and happy show dog when ring time comes, than he would be if he'd spent all morning bracing in fear at the sights around him.

Wire crates, of course, can be covered with canvas covers or draped with towels to give the same privacy, and they have an added advantage of folding flat to fit in car trunks or other crowded places.

Prices are about the same for wire or fiberglass crates, so what you drive may be the deciding factor here. But do get a crate. The dog will need it to rest in on dog show day, and you'll need a safe place to park him while you shop the vendor booths or have lunch or attend to any other matters.

Some people are surprisingly thoughtless of their dogs' comfort, making them ride in open, wire crates on bare metal floor trays, in swaying vehicles, for extended periods, with no padding between hard metal and delicate hocks and elbows, and no traction against sliding back and forth with the motion of the car. Don't be one of those! Old towels are fine for bedding if your dog is destructive, and can be had for pennies at garage sales. Catalogs and vendor booths offer beautiful crate pads that are soft, comfortable, and machine washable. Or watch remnant tables at carpet stores for remnant carpet samples or cheap lengths of that thick fleecy stuff that looks like sheepskin.

Grooming Tables

Most exhibitors also own grooming tables. Even if yours is a large breed, it will be easier to groom him if he's standing on a table. Tables for large breeds are fitted with short legs; tables for Toy breeds stand tall, to save backaches. Grooming tables all fold down for traveling, and have, or can be fitted with, metal grooming arms that curve up over the dog's neck and serve as an anchor. A grooming loop hangs from the arm, or post, and slips over the dog's neck so that he stands reasonably still while you work on him.

With your crate for the dog's escape cave, and your table to work on, you'll be able to stake your claim on precious territory in the grooming/crating area of the show building.

Next on your shopping list, you might want to consider a dolly. Now, be serious. I'm talking about a wheeled platform a few inches above the ground. The dolly is designed to haul your crate, grooming table, folding chairs, cooler, tack bag, and any other miscellaneous articles from your car to the show building and back. Most are made of heavy-gauge wire and have rope or fold-down wire handles, so they weigh only a few pounds and take up little space in the car. Most dog exhibitors depend on their dollies a great deal.

Tack bags or boxes are necessary for all dog exhibitors. You can spend a bundle on specially-made, fancy metal boxes or hand-crafted wooden ones if you like. You can also find something just as good and a whole lot cheaper where housewares are sold. Plastic,

Shopping the vendor booths can be the most enjoyable part of the dog show day. T-shirts are popular items. Even more fun is this booth selling dogs' costumes; clown hats, graduation mortarboards, witches hats, and more.

portable file boxes are nifty if you don't need much room, or nylon carry-all bags, overnight bags, weekend bags, or whatever works for you. My current favorite tack bag is a nylon locker bag designed for sports gear. It's squarish, about a foot wide, eighteen inches deep, and maybe two feet high, with all kinds of pockets and compartments, and a comfortable shoulder strap.

Dryers

You may need a hair dryer, depending on your dog's coat type. If you're going to need to wash feet, faces or any other part of your dog at the show, a dryer *is* a necessity. The same is true if you're showing a coated breed that will need last-minute fluff-drying. For instance, coats of spaniels and setters tend to become stringy-looking fast, unless they are treated with some sort of coat dressing and then blow-dried shortly before showtime. If you show a spaniel or setter, a stringy coat will make you look like a novice. If you're not sure about ring presentation for the appearance of your breed, check with your breeder or others who show the same breed. Take a reading on their opinions of the need for a dryer and proceed accordingly.

You can get an inexpensive hand-held human hair dryer for your tack, or use your own. A midpriced portable dog dryer that will probably be a little more powerful than your personal blow-dryer is another option. You can also get one of the more expensive power dryers, the kind that can blow a small dog off the table if his nails aren't digging in! The power dryers do the job much faster, and will also stretch the coat a bit, especially if it's a kinky coat type. This can be a plus or not, depending on the breed. If your dog is groomed with chalk, a power dryer is the best and fastest way to blow the excess chalk out of his coat before ring time. With any dryer, you'll need electricity. At an indoor show you may have enough outlets to go around, so no problem. At outdoor sites many exhibitors will use small gas generators to furnish their electricity needs. You'll also notice that the experienced person will carry at least one heavy-duty extension cord.

A word of caution here, try not to blow your chalk onto the equipment of the people set up next to you. Grooming areas are usually very crowded, and chalk-storms can get you lynched. Also, be careful not to blow your white chalk all over the black Standard Poodle on the next table.

Other grooming equipment is so breed-diversified that I won't try to tell you what to get, only that it's usually best to spend a little more and get the best quality tools you can find. This is especially true for combs. Cheap combs develop bent and broken teeth faster than hockey goalies. If yours is a scissored breed, again the best bet is the most expensive scissors you can afford. They hold their edge much better than the cheapies, and they do a smoother, more professional job with much less work. Cheap scissors will be in the $20 price range, while top-of-the-line ones can cost ten times as much. There's a happy medium at around $40 to $60.

Leads and Collars

You probably already have one show lead that you've been using for training classes, but when you start going to shows and browsing the vendor booths you'll probably pick up a few more. It's usually best to follow the tradition in your breed—standard slip-clasp show lead, martingale, chain collar, etc. The deciding factor here is whether your dog needs the extra control of a martingale or choke chain, both of which tighten around the dog's throat when he pulls against it. If your dog is powerful and rambunctious this may be a necessity.

If, on the other hand, you want your dog to push against the lead, then you don't want the choke action and a simple slip-clasp show lead is better. Cocker spaniels, for instance, are shown on wide flat fabric leads to encourage them to charge forward against the lead, lowering their hindquarters and sloping their toplines as they push forward. Terriers are often shown on taut leads with much of their weight riding on their throats, so again, choke collars would be wrong unless extra control is necessary.

Some breeds are traditionally shown in the beautiful jewelry-type, fine-link choke chains, called snake chains. A gold snake chain on a gleaming black-and-tan Doberman is striking. But chain collars are bad news for longer-coated breeds because they snag and wear down the coat.

Show leads are available in leather, in slick nylon, in nonslick

66

fabric, in cord-style nylon, you name it. They also come in practically any color. My favorite is the old standard Resco lead, which is nonslick, somewhat stiff, and almost tacky so that it is easy to grip and to wad into a tidy fistful. Slick nylon leads always seem to get away from me and turn into unsightly loops and droops as I'm trying to stack my dog on the judging table, and cord style leads are too hard to hang onto. Leather is great for gripping but can catch against the dog's coat a little more than nylon.

Because show leads are probably the least expensive thing you'll be buying, it's fun to have several and to experiment till you find the one that feels best to you and works best with your dog.

You'll probably also want some sort of apron or grooming smock, so you can work on your dog's coat while keeping your show clothes neat and presentable. Some people enjoy making their own, and adding their kennel names, or sew-on patches showing their breed. You can buy smocks and aprons in vendor booths at shows, order them from kennel supply catalogs, or pick them up at uniform shops selling to beauticians or hospital workers. You can also wear funny chef's aprons that say things like, ''Who invited all these tacky people?'' It's a great area for individual expression.

That First Show

Now you've got your stuff, you've got a reasonably well-prepared dog, and you've got a mailbox full of premium lists. Time to pick a show and enter.

Most dog exhibitors pick shows on the basis of geography, choosing the ones closest to home. As you become more involved, you'll probably expand your territory. You may start out thinking fifty miles is a long way to drive for a dog show, but within a few years that may well have stretched to five hundred. If you live in or near a large city you may find all the shows you want, close to home. If you live in a rural area, especially in the western states, you may have to travel over the horizon, maybe over several horizons to find a dog show.

If you haven't already subscribed to AKC's *Pure-Bred Dogs— American Kennel Gazette,* it is wise to do so. Along with the *Gazette* each month you'll get an Events Calendar, a magazine that lists

This snood is more than a fashion statement, it's protection for long ear feathering that might get dirty or wet before ring time.

every show, nationwide, for the coming months. It lists judging panels and specific assignments at many shows and gives the name and address of the superintendent, and the entry fees. Frequently, it also includes a few generic entry blanks that can be used for any show. So if you spot a show that you'd like to enter, you can fire away without needing a premium list.

You can also buy, at vendor booths at shows, a yearly dog show calendar that gives you an overview of shows in your area. If you're thinking of combining a vacation with a dog show circuit, this calendar will come in handy. However, the calendars don't give entry information, and they aren't always entirely accurate.

As you become more sophisticated you'll probably begin selecting shows for their judges as well as for their location, especially when you have a weekend with a choice of shows. But for starters, you won't know enough about the individual judges to know whom to follow and whom to avoid. So look for a show within your driving range and go for it.

If possible, try to make your debut at a small show rather than an event like Chicago International, Beverly Hills or Philadelphia. Huge shows are huge headaches involving crowds, traffic tie-ups, parking hassles, and more—they are major migraine makers. A small show at some pleasant country fairgrounds, by contrast, will not only result in a happier experience for you, it will also be easier on your dog because, although he doesn't have to do the driving, he does have to be on the receiving end of your transmitted nerve-storms.

Small shows are more friendly. People have more time and space to be helpful to bewildered beginners, and judges have more time to smile, pass pleasant comments, and maybe offer helpful hints about your dog or your handling. At small shows you probably won't have to fight tooth and claw for set-up space in the grooming area or parking space on the grounds.

How can you tell a big show from a small one, you ask. For one thing, the smaller the show, the fewer the judges. Glance through the judging panels listed in the Events Calendar. If there are twenty judges with four judges splitting the breeds in your group, it's a big show. If there are four or five judges doing the whole thing, it's small. One-day shows are almost always smaller than shows that come two to a weekend. A one-day show is one show all alone on the weekend, with no others close by for the following or preceding days. A map may be necessary to figure out whether it's a one-day show or part of a two-show weekend. A two-show weekend might mean two shows at the same location Saturday and Sunday, or two shows within fifty or a hundred miles of each other. Three-show weekends are becoming popular, too.

A one-day show will attract fewer professional handlers than a two-day affair, and lots fewer than a three-day cluster. There are also four, five, or more shows sometimes lumped together in a big cluster or circuit, and sometimes there are strings of clusters or circuits in, for instance, the New England area, the Deep South, Florida, Kansas-Oklahoma or Wyoming-Montana, to name some examples. These can be great fun for vacation trips. But beware, the more shows there are lumped together, the greater will be the percentage of professional handlers you'll have to contend with. For them, the more shows they can hit at once, the more income. So a small one-day show out in the boondocks is much less profitable for handlers than, say, two or three shows a couple of states away. Good. Let them have the big ones, and do your learning at the little, friendly shows.

Making an Entry

You've chosen your show, and you have the premium list in hand. The entry form is easy enough to fill out; just put down the entry fee, class, dog's name and sex, registration number, date of birth, country of birth, breeder's name, sire and dam, and your own name and address. You should have all of the dog's information on his registration certificate.

If you haven't yet sent in the blue slip to register him, you can still enter in shows by using the registration number on the blue slip, but you will be limited to showing him for only thirty days, from the date of the first show, so you'd better hop to it and send in the blue slip as soon as you can.

When you've filled out the entry form carefully and signed it, send it with a check for the amount of the entry fee to the superintendent at the address listed in the fine print at the top of the entry form. Write on your check the name of the show and your breed.

Let me repeat something that should be obvious but sometimes isn't. The entry goes to the superintendent. It does not go to the show-giving club, or to the show building, or to the post office in the host city. Laugh if you must, but these things do happen.

Another point that bears stressing is the closing date for entries. It will be shown on the front of the premium list or in the Events Calendar. Usually it is a Wednesday two or three weeks before the show. It is absolute. There is nothing in the world more rigid and unforgiving than a closing date. This is to allow the superintendent's staff to set up the judging schedule (no small task by the way), and to print up and mail out the judging schedules, then to print the show catalogs. So you can see why they can't make allowances for late entries.

Some shows have limited entries. This will be noted on the premium list, too, so pay attention. A show's entry may be limited by AKC because of the restrictions of the show building. There may just not be enough room for more than six rings, or the grooming or parking space is inadequate to hold a bigger show. If the limit is 800 dogs, the superintendent will accept the first 800 entries plus any others that arrive in the same mail delivery as number 800. If you plan to enter a limited show, by all means send your entry in as early as possible. Sometimes the show will draw fewer than its limit, in which case it's no problem. Sometimes, however, the limit is reached weeks before closing, and after that, tough luck. Your entry will be returned and you'll have to live with your disappointment.

There are more sophisticated ways of entering dog shows. Today's superintendents have FAX numbers by which you can send a last-minute entry, up to the morning of the closing date, with the help of your credit card. This will cost an additional service charge.

Entry services, either private companies who handle dog show entries, or services offered by the superintendents, by which your dog will be listed in their computer are also available. All you do is phone the service and indicate what show you want to enter. These services are handy for people showing numbers of dogs every weekend, but for the beginner with one dog and only occasional show trips, they are probably not worthwhile.

It pays to read the premium list carefully. It will give directions to the show grounds and sometimes a little map. It will list what trophies, if any, are being offered in each breed. It will include any special restrictions on dogs or exhibitors at the show and will indicate whether or not space is provided for unentered dogs. This is a standard statement. People bring unentered dogs all the time, though they are not supposed to be allowed on the show site.

The premium list may also offer dire warnings about state regulations requiring rabies certificates, or the need for parvo vaccinations. In all my years of showing I've never been asked to produce a rabies certificate, nor have I ever heard of anyone actually checking on these things at a show.

The premium list might announce a puppy match for the night before the show, or a barbeque supper for exhibitors, or a program of speakers, eye clinic, tattoo clinic, or other special program that can be fun and helpful. An eye clinic will feature a veterinarian qualified to make official eye checks for various genetic eye disorders common in some breeds. Tattoo clinics offer a chance to have your dog tattooed with an identification number for a modest charge.

Judging Schedule

About a week before the show you'll receive from the superintendent a judging schedule and exhibitor's ticket. The exhibitor's ticket will list your dog's name and class and armband number, and the judging schedule will tell you what time your breed is scheduled to be in the ring.

The judging in each ring is scheduled in time increments of an hour to an hour and a half, so that there is flexibility but also a usable time frame. No one knows ahead of time how many entries there will be for each breed, so it's impossible to be too rigid in planning a show. Yet everyone needs to know roughly what time to be on hand, hence the hour-sized allotments of scheduled breeds. Also, no one knows ahead of time how many last-minute absentees there will be. An entry of twenty Springers might turn out to be only fifteen that actually show up.

Judging may finish well before the next time increment, giving the judge a break for a rest and a cup of coffee, or a chance for winners during the previous time slot to be photographed. Judging must not begin before the published time, but it may run later, if the judge is behind schedule. So, if your breed is first on the list for judging at 10:00 A.M., it will either start on the dot of ten, or somewhat later, but never before.

A rough approximation is that most judges will do around twenty to twenty-five dogs an hour. If your breed is scheduled for the 10:00 A.M. time slot, but *after* fourteen Afghans, you'll be up at around 10:30, probably.

At any rate the judging schedule you'll receive will tell you, closely enough, what time to be there, and also what ring you're showing in.

It also tells you the total number of dogs of your breed entered, and how many class dogs and specials of each sex. You'll see something that looks like 3-6-1-1. That means three class dogs, six class bitches, one male Special, and one bitch Special. From this information you can determine how many points will be available and whether there is a possible major for a breed win over both specials. Then, if your dog already has all his minor points, you'll know ahead of time that there will not be a major available at this show, and you can make your plans accordingly, to go anyway or skip the show entirely.

If yours is a groomed breed, this last week is the time to attend to as many final details of presentation—do as much trimming, stripping—as possible. Remember though, conditioning show dogs is an ongoing process; often the best-prepared dog has the best advantage. Make your lists of what *not* to forget to bring, like tack bag, money, judging schedule and show clothes. I knew a forgetful type once who had a bad habit of getting to the show grounds and discovering she'd forgotten a vital something. So for one show she concentrated every bit of her powers on getting to the show with all equipment present and accounted for. At the show she opened the dog's crate; no dog! She'd forgotten to load just one little thing. Eventually packing for shows becomes second nature and you won't need the list. In the beginning it helps, but even veteran dog fans can forget something.

You'll want to bathe your dog either the evening before show day, or perhaps a day or two ahead of time, depending on the coat type. Ask other people in your breed how far ahead of time they prefer to bathe their dogs. Some coats turn into wispy, clinging messes right after a bath. Some dogs get themselves dirty within hours and need to be bathed at the last minute.

Think these things through, make all the decisions you can ahead of time, so the last-minute loading and setting off will be as tranquil as possible. Okay, tranquil is out of the question, but shoot for minimum stress for yourself, your family, and, most importantly, the dog.

And finally the great day dawns!

Carpeting under exercise pens provides a clean surface over parking lot pavement. Here it makes a pleasant area for a French Bulldog and a . . . gargoyle??

7

First Show

LET'S SAY you take my advice and select a small one-day show in a smallish city three hours' drive from home for your debut. You enter your nine-month-old male Basenji in Puppy Dog 9–12, mail your entry off on time, and receive your judging schedule and exhibitor's pass.

Basenjis are scheduled for judging at 8 A.M., after six Vizslas, two Weimaraners, one Wirehaired Pointing Griffon, and four Afghans. There are seven Basenjis entered, three dogs, three bitches, one male special.

Analyzing the Schedule

You are aghast at the early show time, but you'd better get used to it. Superintendents like to schedule the smooth-coated breeds early in the day if possible, because they require less grooming time than the coated breeds. Besides that, breeds within the group tend to be in alphabetical order. Often you'll find Basenjis first up in the hound breeds, because the Afghans will have been scheduled later to allow grooming time, or the Afghans may have been assigned to a different judge with a larger ring.

You'll notice that a total of twenty dogs has been scheduled for your 8:00 to 9:00 time slot, with Basenjis last in the line. That means that you should be judged at around 8:40 to 8:45, but don't count on it. Take a closer look at the breeds ahead of you.

Six is a big entry for Vizslas in some places, and the breakdown here is 0-5-1-0. An entry of five bitches is probably a major, so it looks as though some Vizsla people got together and built a bitch major; thus the chances are good that they'll all be there. But the breakdown in Weimaraners is 1-1-0-0, or one class dog, one class bitch, no specials. There's a good chance that the dog and bitch will be absent because there will be no points to win, in either sex. The same applies to the Griffon; the breakdown is 0-1-0-0, only one class bitch, no points, and not much hope of winning anything on the Group level with a class bitch, so she, too, may very well be absent.

This shrinks your time factor considerably. The five Vizslas may all be in the Open class, which will take perhaps eight or ten minutes to judge, followed by a quick breed judging with only one special. The Weimaraners are absent, the Griffon is absent and the four Afghans may or may not all be present; then presto, time for the Basenji Puppy Dog class—which is you. If you've dawdled around on the assumption that you won't be going in for another half hour, the judging will go on without you.

Travel Plans

So make your travel plans accordingly. Leave time for traffic delays around the show building because even a small, thousand-dog show is going to mean a host of slow-moving cars, vans and motor homes all converging in the dawn hours and vying for parking space.

You can either leave home at 3:00 A.M., for a planned arrival time of 6:00, or drive over the night before and stay in a hotel/motel. Better yet, since most show buildings have overnight camping facilities if you have a camping vehicle you may choose this alternative. The premium list will tell you whether this show does. If the show is held at a fairgrounds or some other place with earth instead of concrete around it, tents are a possibility. If you have a van, minivan, station wagon, or pickup with camper or shell, feel free to spend the night, sleeping in your vehicle. In most cases the show buildings are open the afternoon and evening before the show, with restroom facilities and sometimes even showers. For overnight parking, the host kennel club or the fairgrounds management may charge you a few dollars. If you use an electrical hookup the charge may be slightly higher. At most shows the average cost for overnight stay with electric hookup is ten dollars.

If you decide on a hotel/motel, be sure to make reservations ahead of time and verify that dogs are allowed. Most premium lists include a listing of hotels/motels near the show site that do allow dogs, but don't take anything for granted. Also be aware that a dog show weekend tends to cause all nearby motels to fill up long before the day of the show.

If you have small children, you might want to leave them with Grandma for the weekend, at least for your first show, and especially if you are the mom. If you're the dad, and Mom will be there to ride herd on them, it's not so important. But if you are Mom and you're trying to get your dog ready, yourself ready, your jitters under control and also have to keep the kids entertained and out of trouble, that can be a lot to ask one person. It will be much easier on you if your mind and hands are free to concentrate on your dog.

So for our hypothetical first show, let's say you have a minivan, you're making the trip alone, and you plan to go the night before and camp in the minivan overnight. It's summer, the show is at a fairgrounds, and you'd rather not spend the money for a motel, so a little roughing-it seems the best alternative. It's better than leaving at 3:00 A.M. for sure.

It's a Sunday show. So you'll spend Saturday morning bathing your dog, packing your minivan and going over your list. You're bringing:

Crate with extra padding in case he messes in there
Dolly
Grooming table with its arm and don't forget the little clamp base for the arm, and the loop.
Folding chair

Tack bag with all the grooming tools you will need and preparations to make your dog as beautiful as he can be, and at least two show leads

Food and water for the dog, food and drink cooler and coffee thermos for yourself

Heavy-duty electric cord

Small portable television set

Small fan

Air mattress, blankets, pillows, towels or something to fasten up over the minivan's windows for privacy

Personal grooming articles

Garment bag with show clothes

Your premium list, judging schedule and exhibitor's pass, and a little extra money to spend in the vendors' booths.

And, oh yes, the dog.

You wave good-bye to your loved ones and sail away on your Big Adventure, and don't laugh at my capital letters. It does feel like a Big Adventure. You tell yourself you don't expect to win anything, but you feel elated anyway. You are a dog show person, off to tilt at windmills and win ribbons!

Arriving at the Site

You find the show grounds with little difficulty. It's late afternoon, but already there are fifteen or twenty assorted motor homes parked around the building. The fairgrounds seem like a complex scattering of structures, some big ones, some open-sided barnlike ones, some little ones that look like food stands or restrooms. But the main activity is centered around the biggest and whitest building—undoubtedly that's where the rings will be.

You drive around until you find a grassy, shady area with electrical outlets mounted on posts every few yards. You park beside one of them and plug in your long cord, running it into the back of the minivan through a window. You test it by plugging in your television set, and find that it is indeed a live outlet. They aren't always, so it pays to make sure before you get too firmly planted.

You walk your dog to get him to relieve himself, and go by

way of the main show building, where you look in to see what's going on. It's a vast echoing interior, and in the center stands a white panel truck with the superintendent's logo on the door. The doors of the truck all stand open; rock music blares from within it. From the back of the truck, T-shirted young men are unloading roll after roll of gray rubber matting, stack after stack of folded lattice fencing. The show rings are taking shape all around the truck.

Along one wall other smaller vans and pickups are unloading the frameworks and stock that will make up the vendor booths. Among the vendors there seems to be a steady flow of joking and news and gripes.

A few people in blue jeans and covered with grime seem to be organizing things and handling problems. A woman sees you and asks in a motherly way if she can do something for you. You smile and shake your head and feel a little out of place, but excited to be here anyway.

Later you find the grooming area and bring your crate, table, and folding chair into the building. Already it is a third full, with clusters of ten or twenty crates and half-a-dozen grooming tables all together. These, you guess correctly, belong to the professional handlers whose mammoth rigs stand outside.

During the evening you and your dog take frequent walks around the grounds, because you're too excited to settle down. Each time you circle the parking area it is more crowded, with camper vans, motor homes and a few tents around the outskirts. People at the rigs are sitting in lawn chairs, watching their dogs in exercise pens, broiling steaks on barbecues, calling back and forth to their neighbors.

You feel a little lonely, a little out of it, but keyed up, too, on the verge of something, a new life, a new collection of friends. Once in a while you stop and visit a bit, when a face looks friendly. You learn almost at once that any dog person will respond to compliments about his dog. You wait for return compliments about your dog, who in your eyes is just as good as any there, but for the most part, the people you talk to would rather talk about their dogs than yours—human nature.

Eventually it grows dark. People disappear into their rigs. In the main building, the rings are set up with their mats and fences,

The night before, when the show building is clean and quiet and peaceful . . .

Until the superintendent's crew arrives and begins setting up the rings.

and judges' tables are draped with kennel club cloths. The vendor booths are all constructed and stocked and covered with tarps for the night. The show committee members have driven off. The grounds are amazingly quiet.

You go back to your van and nest in the pillows and air mattress with your dog in your arms and the little television for company. Sleep is a long time coming.

Your Big Day Dawns

By seven the next morning you are up and ready to go. You wash and dress in the restroom, do your hair in the long restroom mirror with three other women who looked like they also got dressed in minivans. Breakfast is coffee from your thermos and a handful of crackers because nothing else appeals to your nervous stomach. The thought of jelly doughnuts makes you ill.

At 7:00 you take your dog to the grooming building, which has become crowded overnight, and begin work on his coat. There is little to do, but you do it over and over, checking often to see whether your watch has stopped.

At 8:00, unable to stand it any longer, you go to the show building and find Ring two. Just as you enter, the loudspeaker begins to play the national anthem. You turn in the general direction everyone else is facing (the loudspeaker, since there is no flag in evidence) and find yourself oddly moved by the anthem, as though you were about to launch into a patriotic endeavor, instead of competing in a dog show.

Forming Up

Near the entrance to Ring two stands a gaggle of Vizslas, two Afghans, and a few other Basenjis, no Weimaraners, no Wirehaired Pointing Griffon. So you were right to get to ringside early; Basenjis would be up right after the Vizslas and Afghans.

You notice that everyone else is wearing a numbered armband, and panic strikes. At the matches you went to, they gave you your armband at the sign-in table. Then, because you are bright and I brought you up right, the panic abates and you see others getting

Vendor booths are often family projects, and setting up, the night before, is the biggest part of the job. Young son's duty seems to be scattering magazines over the floor.

On show day, some of the most important workers are the sanitary engineers, often recruited from 4-H Dog Project members.

their armbands from the woman sitting at the table near the ring entrance. She wears a badge labeled "Steward." You ease up and listen in while one of the Afghan men says to her, "Open Bitch twelve, please."

Panic returns. You can't remember your armband number. You left your exhibitor's pass back at the van and no one asked you for it when you came in. You edge up to Steward lady and throw yourself on her mercy. "Basenji Puppy Dog but I don't know my number," you croak.

Not to worry, her smile says. Apparently this is old stuff to her. She flips her catalog back to Basenjis, sees only one Puppy Dog entry, shows you the page and sure enough, it's your dog. Seeing his name in the catalog jars you with a jolt of pride. The smiling Steward checks you off as present, hands you your armband and a rubber band to hold it on with, and you step aside to make room for the next guy. Then your hand begins to shake and you can't get the rubber band onto your arm because you are rigidly gripping your dog's lead and can't make your fingers loosen up.

One of the Vizsla women gives you a warm smile and sorts you out.

Only then do you begin to watch what's going on in the ring. A tall, commanding-looking woman is striding back and forth in the center, hands clasped behind her back, frowning at the four red dogs circling the ring at a fast trot. The judge, obviously. She looks as though she's selecting a victim for torture and death, and your heart sinks. You were counting on a jolly judge.

Vizslas zip in and out of the ring so confusingly that your mind blanks and you can't remember a thing about the progression of classes. And suddenly they are replaced by the two Afghans. There were supposed to be four, but only two are in sight. Panic time again. You're up next.

You try to watch the judge to see how she does things, which side of the ring she has the dogs stand at when they first come in, but your mind is floating away again.

A voice behind you says, "Who's your puppy?" You turn to face a middle-aged woman holding two Basenjis' leads and looking down at your dog thoughtfully. You tell her the name of your dog's breeder, and who his sire was. She nods, pinches her lips and mutters something about a soft topline.

You look down at your dog and see that he is indeed standing swaybacked. You panic again. Your beautiful, beloved dog has turned into a pile of garbage before your very eyes, minutes before he has to go into the ring to be scowled at by the Amazon judge with blood in her eye.

Death, where is thy sting?

Another voice behind you, from another Basenji person, mutters, "Don't pay any attention to her, she's trying to psyche you out. He's a lovely puppy."

Show Time!

No time to react. The Afghans are out of the ring, the judge is moving a small table into the center of the ring, and Steward lady is calling out, "Basenji Puppy Dog Five, into the ring."

Your legs turn to water. You need to go to the restroom. You promise God that if he gets you through this you'll be good for the rest of your life. And into the ring you go.

You stand on the mat with your dog before you, forgetting to get down on one knee and stack him as you practiced in training classes and at home. The judge looms into sight, scowling at your dog for an instant while you hurriedly start to kneel to set him up. But before your legs unlock the judge makes a sweeping motion with her hand and says, "Once around and on the table." Her voice sounds human.

Forgetting to wrap your lead neatly in your hand, and tripping twice over the mats, you make the circle and lift your dog awkwardly onto the table. With shaking hands you try to set his legs in place but your nerves are scaring him and he pulls his forelegs back. The judge, impatient at the delay, lifts his chest and swiftly sets his front legs where she wants them.

She hums under her breath as she flips up his lip for a look at his teeth, runs her thumbs over his backskull and wrinkles, and fingers his ears. Her mind seems to be far away as she splays her hands around his body, feels his legs, checks his testicles and finishes with a sliding fist around his curled tail. The tail snaps back tightly into place as her hand releases it. She has said nothing about his soft topline, but those gimlet eyes will have missed nothing.

"Down and back," she says abruptly. She positions herself at the end of the diagonal mat and waits with little patience while you get your dog down off the table and into motion. You try to trot him in a dead straight line out away from her on the diagonal mat, but he seems to want to weave around. The return trip is better. He's heading straight for the ring entrance and seems to be in a hurry to get there.

"Again," the judge barks, and you do it again, somewhat straighter this time.

"Over there," she motions, and you go to stand before the first place placard at the edge of the ring near her table. She writes something in her book, peers at your armband to be sure of the number, and hands you a blue ribbon. "Nice youngster," she says, and . . . smiles!

You float out of the ring, nearly colliding with two women coming in for the Open Dog class, the one who said "soft topline" and the one who said "don't listen." You watch the Open class and grin with extreme pleasure when the nicer of the two women wins it. She stays in the ring.

"Puppy Dog Five," the Steward calls, waving you into the ring. You'd almost forgotten about Winners. The Winners class is you and the nice Open woman. The judge merely has you circle the ring together, then gait individually up and back, then she points to Open Woman and says, "Winners." You start out of the ring but the Steward waves you back, and the not-nice Open woman comes back in to compete with you for Reserve.

This time the judge doesn't look at your dog at all but merely gaits Not-Nice up and back, sends the two of you around the ring together, then points to . . . *you.* "Reserve," she commands, and you obey, grinning foolishly as you accept the ribbon.

"I like him," the judge snaps. "Little more maturity, and you'll do all right with him."

Hugging your dog and your joy, you stand back from the ring entrance and watch the judging of the three bitches, and this time it seems clear about Winners and Reserve and who is supposed to be in the ring. The special comes in, followed by the nice Open woman with her Winners Dog, and a young boy who has just won Winners Bitch. The champion gets Best of Breed, the nice Open woman gets Best of Winners, and the boy gets Best of Opposite Sex.

And suddenly it's all over. You had somehow expected more, but the other Basenji people have faded away, it's not quite 9:00, and it's all over. For a moment, you are swamped with a sort of depression. It all went so fast. All those months of preparation, all the daydreams and hoping and practicing and grooming and being scared, and it was all over in minutes. You have already entered another show but it's two months away, and suddenly you want to be back in that ring again, doing it again. Doing it better. Winning bigger.

You take your dog out into the sunshine, back toward your minivan. Was it worth it, after all? Was having a show dog worth the experience you have just been through? Will it be worth it in the future?

Then the nice Bulldog lady you talked to last night walks past and says, "How'd you do?"

"Reserve out of three," you say and grin, and she congratulates you. "That's good for his first time in the ring. He's a good-looking youngster."

"Welcome to the Club . . ."

Suddenly the cloud lifts and the joy starts pouring in. You put your dog away for a rest, haul your stuff out of the grooming building and get it loaded, then go back into the building to shop at the vendor booths and to watch the judging. You notice a Basenji in a ring full of dogs of all breeds, and go closer to check it out.

It is Junior Showmanship competition, and the boy in the ring is the one who had Winners Bitch. You recognize his mother as the nice Open woman, and you sit down beside her. She smiles, says a few nice things about your dog, asks you where you're showing next, then begins to tell you in detail about every Basenji she has ever owned.

Welcome to the club; you are now a dog show exhibitor.

8

Looking Like a Pro

THE POINT OF THIS BOOK is to help you past the novice level of the dog show world, so you can begin getting maximum enjoyment out of the whole thing as soon as possible. Although you may be assuming the role of blithely uncaring beginner, no one really likes being on the bottom rung of any social structure.

Time alone will make a genuine difference in your status, but while you are developing tenure there are things you can do to assure that you look and feel as professional as possible, as soon as possible. So sit up and pay attention now, here comes a whole chapter full of good advice for you, some of which you might even utilize.

Your Image

First, take a good look at yourself, your physical appearance in the show ring, as compared to the better professional handlers. The goal you should be aiming for is unobtrusive neatness, clothes that don't detract from your dog, clothes that work well in the show ring. No

Your clothing on show day is your dog's backdrop. This pair will be an eye-catching picture in the Giant Schnauzer ring.

one cares if you aren't gorgeous (thank God) or if you're over-
weight or unusually short or tall or many things that might seem
important in other areas of your life. But you and your dog are seen
as a team, and you will make an impression on the judge when he
first glances at you, for better or for worse.

For women, hair is likely to be a factor. Style isn't important;
neatness is. If you ordinarily wear your hair in a giant frizzy bush or
in long lanky tresses, consider corralling it for the occasion in a
ponytail or braid, anything to keep it from hanging and swinging
and detracting from the picture. You won't want to need your hand
to get your hair out of your eyes just when you need both hands to
set up your dog.

Makeup should be minimal, or at least not obvious. You want
the judge to focus on the dog—not on you.

Dress to Win

Clothing should be neat and uncluttered, machine washable and
wrinkle-free, with enough leg room to allow free movement around
the ring, but not so much fullness that the outfit flaps around and
spooks your dog or makes him veer out away from you when you
gait him. Pockets are mandatory. Skirt length can be anything you
feel and look good in, but bear in mind that when you kneel behind
your dog to set him up on the floor, short skirts can reveal a whole
lot more than you realize. This also applies to low, loose necklines
when you bend over your dog to stack him.

Of course some exhibitors deliberately dress in a provocative
manner, with the notion that it helps. Usually it does not, but it's far
better not to try to get your wins that way, nor to look as though
that's the game you're playing.

For women, the choices are wide: skirt and blouse or sweater,
dress, jumper, suit, dressy pantsuit. For men the choices are more
limited but easier: dress pants, suit or sport jacket, shirt and tie. You
may find local or breed traditions to follow, shooting jackets in
some sporting breeds, for instance.

Shoes are important, but not as fashion statements. They need
to have soft soles with good traction, comfortable fit and no high-

Men professional handlers and serious amateurs wear suits or sport coats in the show ring. Women of equal status dress with equal care. To do less is to insult your judge.

heels or open toes. The prevailing footwear is tennis shoes. My preference is thick-soled loafers.

Jeans are never acceptable. I don't care if you wear them to church and work and everywhere else. In the show ring, they will make you look like an ignorant beginner. Worse, they will send a message to the judge saying that you didn't think this was an important enough occasion to change into something nicer. This is perceived as a tiny but definite insult to the judge.

It can be fun to develop a signature look for yourself. I like a solid-color look, a silk blouse with skirt of a matching or harmonizing color that makes a pretty background for my dogs. Young Bedlingtons go through a dingy brownish coat stage in adolescence, so I'm careful not to wear blues then, since blue makes them look even more off-color.

You can experiment at home, by going through your closet and holding various garments up to your dog. You'll probably find some colors that make him look extra sharp.

Some people like using a signature color. I know a woman who always wears purple when she shows, in hopes of subliminally suggesting the purple ribbon to the judge. I once knew a man who brought various outfits to shows, checked to see what his judge was wearing that day, then dressed as nearly like the judge as possible. He claimed it helped him win. I don't know about that.

As you get to know judges, though, you may want to trim your sails to the prevailing winds a bit. Some older, more conservative judges have never approved of women wearing slacks in the show ring. Elegantly dressed, older women judges may be put off by flimsy, flowing, flowery stuff and excess eye makeup.

You will know you've graduated from novice status when you can go into a dress shop and explain to the clerk that you need a chocolate brown A-line skirt with deep pockets but it can't be too yellowish or it will clash with your dog—without feeling silly.

One final clothing check here; test your show outfit to see if anything flaps or droops when you bend over your dog to set him up. Men's ties that aren't tacked down, for instance, or massive necklaces or scarves. And if you're wearing a straight or short skirt, check to see what happens in the rear when you bend over. You may be entertaining the troops at ringside more than you know.

Act Like a Winner

Enough about clothes, now let me pick on the rest of you for a while. How do you hold your lead? This may have been covered for you in your training classes, but a little more nagging couldn't hurt, especially since this is a point at which novices really look like novices, and it's so easy to correct.

Two points here, no flapping ends, and no upside-down holds. No matter what style lead you use, the excess can and should be folded, rolled, or otherwise contained so that you use only the length that you need to control your dog and everything else is out of sight. Next, make sure the lead is coming out of the bottom of your hand, by your little finger, *not* out of the top, by your thumb. This is a weak, awkward position that looks bad and stamps you as a beginner.

Equestrians are taught, from the first, that the reins must always come into the fist at the bottom, and for good reason. In this position a straight line is formed from the rider's elbow to the horse's mouth, and a straight line is much more powerful than a zigzag line. If the rein zigzags from bit to top of hand, down through hand, and out the bottom and on to the elbow, the hand becomes a hinge, a weak link because of the flex of the wrist.

It's exactly the same with a dog lead going from the pull of a fifty-pound dog to the anchor of the elbow. Even on small, light-weight dogs when strength isn't the issue, the correct hand position just looks better. It's one of the first things judges penalize Junior Showmanship kids for.

Arm position. Up and out, with your hand at about chest height, your elbow semistraight but with a relaxed bend.

Now, where are you and your dog in relation to the mat? You in the middle and the dog slipping on the bare floor or crowding in too close to you? Wrong. The dog should be centered as nearly as possible on the mat, with you off to the edge if necessary. If there's room for both of you without getting the dog too near the edge, fine. If not, the dog comes first. The whole idea is to allow your dog to move in a free and unencumbered way so the judge can see and evaluate his movement as it really is. If the poor dog has to "crab" or sidewind in between the mat edge and your flapping, swirling skirt he's likely to hang back or do something else that will make him look bad unnecessarily.

Now let's pick on your posture for a while. The tendency for all of us is to curve forward and to the side, sticking our faces in front of the dog to make sure he's moving okay. Of course this makes us look like Notre Dame bellringers and can lead to crashes with ring fencing or rear-ending the guy ahead of us. Besides, it tends to make the dog slow down. It is much better to carry yourself proudly erect, confident smile on your face, watching your dog from the edge of your vision if you must, but sailing forth radiating assurance. Fake it if you must.

Facial expression can give away more than you'd like. It may be harder to control your face than body position, but try anyway. If your face is stiff with fear the judge will know you're a beginner, and may not respect your entry as much as she would if you came into her ring looking as though you were an old hand at this and had been winning every time out. A relaxed smile, if you can produce it, is the best advantage you can give yourself aside from a good dog.

How should you respond to the judge? React as pleasantly and naturally as you can manage. Bear in mind that judges really are human. They respond to a warm smile just like other people. It's best not to be chatty. While the judge is examining your dog his mind is supposed to be on what he's seeing and feeling, not on passing the time of day with you. If you have a good dog you want the judge to have time to discover that fact.

This is absolutely not the time to drop messages about other wins the dog has had, or who his sire is or his breeder. That sort of thing is verboten by the rules, and falls into the category of cheap and obvious tricks that most judges will see through anyhow, and dislike you for.

When you lose, it's a nice gesture to quickly congratulate the winner, especially if it's someone you know. For strangers it's not expected, unless it's an especially exciting win, like finishing a champion.

When you win, it's best to accept your dog's success with a happy smile but not with screams and leaps and expressions of breathless wonderment. That only tells the world you're not used to winning. And it doesn't endear you to those you just beat, who may be fighting crushing disappointment as they leave the ring. Save your whooping for the privacy of your car with the windows rolled up!

Other novice habits to overcome are crowding up too close behind the exhibitor in front of you, and not paying attention to when you should be entering and exiting the ring.

Photo Opportunities

You'll have noticed by now that many people have pictures taken after they win. The photography sessions usually occur at the end of each time segment, when the judge has a little extra time before judging the next scheduled breed. If you want to get a picture, mention it to the ring steward as you leave the ring, then hang around at ringside until you see the photographer come into the ring and start setting up. There will usually be a few other exhibitors getting pictures, so just jump in and take your turn.

When is it customary to do a photo? Novices, which you are trying not to look like, will sometimes get photos of very small wins, first place in the puppy class, in an entry of one, or Reserve out of three. These are something of a nuisance to the judge, who is taking time from his break or lunch period, or who may be behind in his judging schedule and already late in starting his next breed.

Photos of the dog's first major win, or first breed win over specials, something memorable early in his career, and then others when he finishes his championship are appropriate. If my dog goes on to a specials career I'll often get pictures of Group placements, especially if it's a judge I particularly like, or a pretty showgrounds with a mountain range in the background, or an impressive trophy.

The photographer will know who you are by your armband number or by the win. He has marked catalogs, so he can find the name and address of every winning exhibitor. Photographers differ, but most will automatically send you a color 8″ × 10″ along with a bill for it. You don't have to buy the photo if you don't like it, just return to sender. If you want extra prints, there will be an order form enclosed.

Some exhibitors use that photography session to chat up the judge, make an impression so the judge will better remember them

94

next time around. Judges aren't fools. They know what's going on. Some exhibitors send copies of photos to the judge on the same motive. There may be memorable wins that would have meaning for the judge as well as for you, and in that case you might ask the judge, while the picture is being taken, whether he'd like a copy. But don't expect your tiny victory to be a peak moment in the judge's life.

Ask and Learn

A couple of habits brand novices as novices, indiscriminate advice-seeking and indiscriminate bragging. Try to watch out for this two-headed evil.

Advice-seeking is okay. You learn by asking questions and that's fine, so long as you're asking the right people. The breeder you bought your dog from is the first and usual source of help about things like grooming, training, when to start showing and what judges to seek or avoid. But maybe your breeder is less than helpful, or doesn't really know that much. Then you have to go looking for other sources. This can get tricky.

If you declined to buy the puppy that Breeder A offered you, then turned around and bought from Breeder B, then A isn't likely to have a warm spot in her heart for you, and if you go to her expecting help with your new puppy, that's asking quite a bit of human nature. If you eschewed all the local breeders and brought in a dog from another part of the country, ask not what the local folk can do for you, because they could be out to plow you under. They'll want to teach you the error of your ways, and certainly they will not feel like giving you grooming tips. You are the competition.

Now, in some cases these will be nice people, they won't hold your not buying from them against you—at least not much—and some may offer you help and advice. Use your own judgment here. Don't be too surprised if the advice they give turns out to be deliberately wrong. "Enter under So-And-So, he'll like your dog," so you enter your oversized dog under him and the helpful competition smirks as they walk away with the win, with their tiny dogs, and you find out later that the judge never puts up big ones.

Okay, shame on them for leading you astray, but shame on you, too, for walking into it.

This is a highly competitive sport, and everyone hangs his ego as well as his heart on his own dogs. There is always an element of insult when you choose another breeder or bloodline to buy from, and that little insult will set up a slightly combative spirit in the others you'll be showing against. In popular breeds this won't be much of a factor because there are lots of dogs and people and breeders and bloodlines, but in rarer breeds, if you bypass the locals and go elsewhere, it's understandable that these people may not be wishing you well when you begin showing.

For the most part they will be pleasant enough, even helpful in small ways, but don't go to them expecting, for instance, grooming help that might mean your dog beating theirs in close competition.

Often it's a better plan to strike up acquaintances in breeds with coats similar to your dog's, and ask for advice from them as to what kind of coat dressing they use, or blow dryer, or whatever. You can also learn from others in your breed by setting up near them in the grooming area and keeping an eye peeled as to what they are spraying on or snipping off.

No One Likes a Blowhard

Indiscriminant bragging is another earmark of the novice, and a particularly obnoxious one. You may believe that your dog is superior and wonderful and the best that ever lived, and it's okay to feel that way, so long as you don't try to shove it down the throats of everyone around you. Always remember and never forget, as someone on television used to say, those people who are smiling glassy-eyed while you brag on and on about your dog, feel the same way about their own, and maybe with more reason.

Most dog people are pretty patient about listening to the tyro brag about his dog winning third in a class of five, repeating every syllable the judge uttered about the dog's potential, and every ringside compliment from admiring watchers. But they do reach a saturation point. Try to bridle your tongue before your audience goes cross-eyed, will you?

One of the first facts you should learn about dog people is that we all, every one of us, are primarily focused on our own dogs. We're willing to humor the chatty novice for a while as she brags about wins we ourselves would have considered defeats. But we get tired of the subject very quickly. What we really want, of course, is to brag about our own dogs.

The Perpetual Novice

We've been talking about ways you can avoid looking and sounding like a beginner, but there's another side to this picture, the temptation to go on playing the role of novice indefinitely.

It's tempting in some ways. Everyone likes novices because they are little threat in the show ring, because they make admiring audiences, because they tend to be humble and excited and somewhat, well, submissive. They don't threaten anyone, therefore they are welcomed into the pack and generally treated cordially.

It's only when they begin to have opinions of their own in conflict with others, and when they begin to win regularly, that the little animosities can start to form. Some people choose not to take that upward step, but to stay in the role of humble novice permanently. They never have very good dogs, never win much, never seem to learn anything, and to all outward appearances they go on year after year having a fine time at the dog shows. They don't make enemies within their breed because they never have strongly held convictions, never stand up for anything, never speak out.

Maybe this is what is right and comfortable for them, and that's fine.

But if you want to earn your way up in the dog world, you'll have to be prepared to leave the security of the perennial beginner pose, and let your confidence and ability grow. You may not make or keep as many friends, but they will probably be more genuine and more worthwhile.

Earning Your Spot

Dog peoples' respect must usually be earned. However, if you are out there with a good dog, doing a polished job of presenting him, taking wins and losses with equal grace, and keeping your mind open to the continual learning process, most people you come to know in the dog show world will gradually begin to respect you.

And when you are that kind of exhibitor, believe me, the pleasures multiply.

Respect is worth working for.

9

Playing Politics

"DOG SHOWS ARE SO POLITICAL." You'll hear that over and over, if you haven't already. Is it true? What does it mean?

Good questions.

Let me evade the answers for a minute while we look at who runs things in the dog show world, so you can have an overview of where the powers lie.

The American Kennel Club

On top of the power pyramid is of course the American Kennel Club, the ruling body in the world of purebred dogs. This is a large, not-for-profit organization with its main headquarters in New York City and registration department in Raleigh, North Carolina.

The AKC performs a wide range of functions within the dog fancy. It sets the rules and enforces them. It grants approval to judges and gives permission for local clubs to hold shows and matches. It provides an official representative for most shows to

A quiet moment before going into the fray.

answer questions and settle disputes. It takes a small percentage of all entry fees, records point wins and issues championship certificates. AKC registers litters and individual dogs, and records changes of ownership. And it stands as judge and jury in complaints against judges, fellow exhibitors, and show committees.

It grants, suspends, or revokes the right of an individual to register or exhibit dogs at AKC shows.

Of course, AKC regulates field trials and other performance events, but for our purposes show-related activities are the germane functions.

Part of the AKC's role in dog shows is to protect the judges' omnipotence. Within his or her ring a judge is supreme, and AKC backs judges almost entirely. Although this policy is considered necessary to the sport in theory, it can create bad situations for exhibitors. For instance, a judge may be deliberately or unintentionally rude to exhibitors, whereas any degree of rudeness from exhibitor to judge would mean instant dismissal from the ring and even the possibility of suspension of all AKC privileges for the exhibitor.

AKC inspectors can come into a breeder's kennel at any time, without warning, inspect the records and identification of dogs, and slap large fines or suspensions on any breeder who refuses him access, or whose records are not up to snuff. This is for the purpose of cleaning up puppy mill activity, and it may do some small good in that area, but it can be quite intimidating to breeders in general because all the power is on one side.

Judges

Next in the power chain is the judge. He or she is approved by AKC to judge one specific breed, or several breeds, or an entire Group, or any number of breeds and Groups. The top of the hierarchy is the small group of judges approved to judge all breeds. On another plane altogether is the specialty judge with approval for one or two breeds.

At this time there are around 3,000 approved judges in the United States, only some twenty of whom are empowered to judge all breeds.

Thoughtful judges will be considerate of dogs and handlers in hot weather, and allow them to wait in the shade. This is especially important for breeds like Bulldogs, who have some difficulty breathing in very hot weather, and overheat easily.

Anyone who meets certain qualifications can apply for approval to judge any breed or breeds he or she wishes. Most first-time applicants will usually apply for one breed, perhaps two. The qualifications include passing written tests, having a sufficient, documented background in dogs, and having judged a few matches, sweepstakes and futurities and having stewarded. The prospective judge's application must undergo AKC review and the applicant's name and breed applied for must be published in the *Gazette* for fancier input. If all hurdles are cleared and provisional approval is granted, he must judge five times on a provisional basis, but he is not allowed to "solicit" judging assignments. Of course he must solicit a little, passing the word to friends in various kennel clubs for instance, in order to get those necessary judging jobs which will move him from provisional judge status to regular judging approval. It's hard to get one-breed judging assignments because they aren't very practical for the host club.

Next, if he wants to become a full-time professional judge, making his living judging dog shows, he must add as many other breeds as possible and fast as possible until he has an entire variety (Sporting, Working, etc.) group, then a second group and so on. In order to be approved for these additional breeds, he must keep adding judging assignments. This requires considerable networking, making as many friendly contacts as humanly possible in as many show-giving clubs as possible, and being perceived as an asset to any judging panel.

Even with massive networking efforts it takes most judges years to acquire enough breed approvals to ensure a steady income. The more breeds one is approved to judge, the greater is one's potential judging income. But in order to accomplish all this you have to somehow get the assignments.

Judging assignments are obtained by knowing the right people and by getting those right people to want you on their judging panels. In each kennel club there are a few key people, sometimes only one or two individuals, who make most of the judge selection decisions year after year. Judges know who these key people are. They study exhibitors like we study them, and they have as active a grapevine for exchanging information about kennel club power-holders as exhibitors have about which judge puts up which handlers.

We're all out there pursuing our own goals, and fairly often those goals can be mutually met from opposite ends. Here's a likely scenario. A key kennel club member has a Norwegian Elkhound that she's been handling herself and specialing with no success at all. She's getting frustrated at her lack of wins on the Group level. Comes the time for her club to select its slate of judges for next Spring's show and she decides to help herself.

She's a friend of a friend of a man who has recently been approved to judge all breeds in the Hound group. He's not well known, and he's hungry for judging assignments. Her club's show chairman gives her the green light to offer him the job, since the chairman shows Sporting dogs and can be noncommittal.

Ms. Elkhound finds a show where Mr. Houndjudge is doing Elkhounds, and she enters under him. It's a small show, she has the only special and he gives her the breed win. She has a win picture taken, using this opportunity to chat him up, make an impression on him so that he'll remember what she looks like, then drops a hint that she'll be calling him soon about a judging assignment.

A few days later, before he's had time to forget what she looks like, she calls and offers him the job, which he takes gratefully. She sends him a copy of the win picture with him and her dog and her, just to be sure he doesn't forget her face.

Her show won't happen for almost a year yet, but meanwhile he owes her one. She watches the judging panels in each month's *Events Calendar* until she finds a small show, away from major handlers, in which Mr. H. is judging Elkhounds and the Hound group. The show is a two-day drive, but it's worth it. She makes the trip and goes to his ringside early in the day for a brief hello while he's waiting for his judging assignment to begin. After a second or two her face clicks in his mental file and he remembers that she's the one who got him the Hound Group assignment at Nonesuch next May. He smiles.

Surprise surprise, her dog wins the breed. Surprise surprise, he goes on to a Group second. Her dog is a nice one, she's done a good job of presenting him, she's not a famous professional handler, nothing seems amiss. Other exhibitors congratulate her warmly. She has the photo of the win published in several dog magazines, and gradually other Group level wins begin to come her way.

Next May at the Nonesuch show she is assigned the job of meeting Mr. H.'s plane at the airport and driving him to his hotel and picking him up in the morning for the drive to the show grounds. They get acquainted and launch a minor but friendly relationship that may well lead to more wins in the future. She does not show that day, because it's her own club and that might seem in poor taste. She stewards for Mr. H. instead, seeing that he has coffee when he wants it and that his classes come into the ring in the order he prefers.

By the end of the day they are friends and she can be reasonably sure that Mr. H. will be kindly disposed at future shows toward her and her dog.

What's wrong with this picture?

The man did a decent job of judging that day, so the club wasn't hurt. The woman's dog was of competitive quality and may have deserved the Group second. So where is the harm? This scenario shows business as usual in the dog show world. This is the way in which most beginning judges must play the game in order to get the assignments necessary to further their careers.

The harm, of course, is that four or five other dogs in the Hound group that day were more deserving of the win than the Elkhound; they had nothing going for them except their quality, and went home empty-handed. Their owners had no idea what was behind the judge's decisions.

Professional Handlers

Next, let's take a look at professional handlers. These are men and women who make all or part of their living by showing other peoples' dogs for a fee. Handlers often operate in husband-wife teams, and usually with an entourage of helpers. Many also have boarding kennels, grooming shops, or both. It's a tough business to break into and even tougher to succeed in. The faint-hearted need not apply.

There was once licensing of handlers by AKC but not anymore. There are no official controls over the profession. Anyone who wants to can call himself a handler and charge whatever fees he wishes. Handlers range from the hobby exhibitor who shows an extra dog or two for his friends to help with show expenses, to the major handlers whose income can be considerable.

Handlers' fees vary widely and keep going up, but just as an example, let's invent another of our fictitious characters and say that Miss Handler charges a flat $60 fee, plus ten cents a mile traveling expenses from her home to the show and back. If she takes your dog to Best of Breed, and picks up a Group fourth, that's good for a twenty dollar bonus. Group third brings thirty, Group second forty, and Group first is worth fifty dollars to the winning handler. For a Best in Show, a two hundred dollar bonus is usual, but a Best at a very big, important show can bring more.

In addition, she's charging you a per day rate between shows to board and "condition" your dog. This can mean that your dog may spend too much time in a crate with minimal exercise and attention, other than keeping his coat in show shape, while in the handler's care.

If you decide to hire a handler, know in advance what you are expected to pay and what your money entitles you to. Inspect the handler's facilities and get references. As in any other service business some are better than others. It's your dog and your money so choose wisely.

Unfortunately, some handlers become adept at performing illegal cosmetic surgery that picks up where Nature left off. A private session in the handler's motor home can correct a gay tail, a flying ear, a crooked bite, a missing testicle. The dogs suffer. The handler profits, and a month later the dog is in the ring and winning. This regrettable situation would not exist if owners of these dogs refused to play along.

Subtract the overhead expenses, which might include running and paying for a sizable motor home and one or two minimum-wage salaries, feed bills and utility bills for the kennel at home, and you still have a pretty nice income for Miss Handler. If she can by whatever means elevate herself to the ranks of "clout" handler, she can double or triple the income from the same number of dogs. Clout handlers are those who frequently win Groups and Bests, and can finish almost any dog to its championship because of their own profiles. They can charge breathtaking fees because their clients hire them to win—plain and simple!

How does she enter the exalted ranks? Winning is the magic

ingredient. By building a reputation for finishing dogs whose owners' efforts were unsuccessful, she develops a following. By making many trips to the winners' circle, she attracts the favorable attention of clients and judges.

A major handler might carry an average string of fifteen to thirty dogs. This represents a fair amount of entry money for the host club, which makes its money from show entry fees. Judges who are unpopular with handlers do not draw the handler-entries. Judges who can't draw sizable entries find it hard to land judging assignments, because the host clubs need the entries to break even on their shows.

Miss Handler therefore is in a position to help Mr. H.'s judging career along by showing under him whenever she can, and bringing him large entries. This in turn makes him look good to other clubs who are thinking about hiring him. These two are in a position to help each other get where they want to go, Mr. H. to more and better judging assignments and perhaps eventual all breed status, and Miss Handler to more and bigger wins, a bigger reputation as a sure-fire win-getter for her clients, higher income, better dogs to choose from and richer clients to underwrite the dogs' careers. Lavish ads in slick dog magazines, showing Miss Handler with her top-ranked show dogs, will surely lead to more and wealthier clients.

Now, along the way Mr. H. may gain a reputation as a handler's judge, one who tends to put up handlers even when an owner-handled dog is patently better. This reputation won't really hurt him, though. The owner handler with the better dog hasn't cultivated an image, and is just an anonymous face.

Mr. H. may be a good judge and a decent man who is just doing what he has to do to succeed in his profession. He may feel badly about the good owner-handled dog he just dropped, and if he has a chance to put that dog up at another show, he may well give it a little better win than it deserves, feeling, rightly or wrongly, that he owes it.

Owner-Handlers

The last and least powerful group in the lineup is the average owner-handler. That's you. Sorry.

There is little we can do to change the political structure of the dog show world so, assuming we are essentially honest folk who just enjoy showing the dogs we love, we have to make some choices. Usually this point comes after a year or two of showing, when we've begun to realize how the cards are stacked.

Here are the choices. We can opt out and simply quit showing. We can look for other arenas such as obedience or tracking. We can decide to play the game by the existing rules and start looking for ways to get a foothold in the power structure, such as getting on show committees and hiring our own pet judges. Or we can trim our sails to the prevailing winds and find ways to enjoy the sport while maintaining our dignity.

Yes. It can be done. Here are a few ways.

Set realistic goals. If you enjoy matches but get too tense and angry at shows, then spend your weekends going to fun matches. Write to every kennel club in your traveling range and ask to be put on their mailing list for flyers for their next match. Forget championships as a goal and instead, go for the fun of competing and winning on a lower level. Go for the fun of having your dog admired, and the pleasure of being with people you like.

If that seems artificial to you, not quite the real thing, then go showing by all means, but choose your judges carefully. Keep notes on every judge you show under or hear comments about, and don't walk your dog into no-win situations. If your dog is of comparable quality to the others in his breed in your area, and if you're doing a good job of presenting him, he will get his share of the wins under the better judges. But if he can't ever seem to get the points, then try setting your hopes on getting a nice placement in the classes rather than on winning the points.

If your goal is to campaign a Special and you think your dog is good enough, then do it, but do it right. Get him out every weekend, travel where you must, keep records of judges, enter where you have at least a reasonable chance at a breed win or Group placement. Do the magazine ads to promote your dog. Know ahead of time that it's going to be expensive and decide where your priorities lie. Know what your dream will cost, then pay or change dreams.

If you're not deeply committed to your breed, and it's a popular breed, consider changing to a similar one in which it may be easier to win. Many people do just that.

When you walk into a political situation and have to swallow an undeserved defeat, take it quietly, hang onto your dignity, and just be sure you don't walk into it again. If it's become obvious to one and all that Mr. H. always puts up Miss Handler in Whippets even when she's showing mediocre ones, then make a note of that and don't enter your Whippet Special at shows where Miss Handler is likely to appear. If Mr. H. and Miss H. have something going between them, let it be on their consciences, but don't play into it. Find another show to go to that weekend, or stay home and paint the garage.

Get to know the show string of the handler you need to avoid, and earmark one obvious entry. If he handles a Griffon Special, it's likely to be the only Grif being specialed in your area because the breed is so rare. Enter two different sets of shows on a given weekend if you want to, and then when the judging schedule comes, check to see which shows have a male Griffon Special listed . . . and go to the other show instead. If he isn't carrying a rare breed Special, you'll have to wing it!

Work on getting better and better dogs, and doing a more expert job of presenting them. It does pay off, and you will increase your win ratio.

Work on making yours a familiar face, if only to a few of your favorite judges. Go out of your way to show under them, greet them with a smile of recognition. They may not know you from Adam's off ox, but if you repeatedly show up in their rings radiating a positive image and showing good dogs, eventually they will begin to respond. They will remember you from one show to the next, and to lean more and more in your direction in close decisions.

Ask questions of as many knowledgeable exhibitors as you can about individual judges, and by all means keep notes. Most judges develop reputations of one kind or another, and frequently they are soundly based, but not always. If you talk to only one source, you might hear that Mr. H. always puts up small dogs, or dark dogs, or women exhibitors. This espionage might be based on one show at which Mr. H. happened to put up a small, dark dog handled by a woman.

If you hear the same things from several sources, though, they are probably true. For instance, some judges are considered movement judges. If your dog excels in movement but has a common head, this could be a good judge for you to try. Some judges love cute, little bitches. Some love a big, impressive animal and will put up an oversized bitch when they shouldn't have just because, to them, substance equals quality.

Many judges are impressed with coat and will put up the dog with the thickest or longest coat, even though the breed standard calls for the opposite.

Some are very clearly "handler" judges, while others seem to enjoy placing owner-handled dogs. Some blatantly put up their personal friends, or friends of friends. Many judge with an eye to furthering their own careers and will lean toward the exhibitor who might throw a judging assignment their way.

I tend to be leery of showing against a competitor who belongs to the same kennel club as the judge, or who has bought or bred dogs from the judge's line, or has other such visible ties. I might try once or twice, to give him the benefit of the doubt, but I don't go on playing into an obvious situation. Nor should you.

The more you know about the judges you enter under, the better you can protect your own tail feathers.

There are good judges out there, believe me. The species is alive and well. There are judges who work very hard at finding the best dog in every class, and placing their dogs in strict order according to their perception of quality, regardless of who is on the other end of the lead.

It is very possible for a knowledgeable owner handler with good dogs to do quite well, and to win more than enough to keep the sport fun and exciting. Many of us are out there doing it every weekend. We might not be as visible or as vocal as the disgruntled losers, but we're there and we're having fun.

What's the Real Perspective on Politics?

Are dog shows political? Sure they are. But they are less so than horse shows, I believe, because the personal connections between judges and exhibitors are fewer, and because there is less money involved.

110

But the situation is tailor-made for little corruptions. Okay, big ones, too. If we define political judging as any in which factors other than the relative qualities of the dogs enter into the awards, then yes, it happens a lot.

Some judges don't know much about the breed and feel safe putting up the recognizable professional handler on the theory that it must be a good dog or Miss H. wouldn't be handling it.

Some judges are honest and knowledgeable about most breeds but don't know much about yours, or they are tired or hung over or have sore feet, and therefore skim through your breed doing the easy things in order to get on to the lunch break. They'll automatically put an Open entry over a puppy, Winners Dog over Winners Bitch, male Special for breed and bitch Special for Best Opposite—takes no effort. Some judges get careless or tired and simply place them in the order they stand, coming around the ring. Less effort is involved than sorting out the best dog.

Some judges put up faces that they've been seeing in ads in the dog magazines sent free to all judges. For this competitive edge, owners pay hundreds of dollars a month for photos and ads.

Some judges put up handlers because they used to be handlers themselves. They know it's a tough way to make a living, they know that a Group placement for a handler is extra income whereas the same Group placement for an amateur is just a ribbon, so old-boy loyalty sways them toward giving the win where it will mean the most, income-wise.

Some judges put up the exhibitors who support them with entries. An owner-handler who routinely brings such a judge four or five entries every time he judges in her area will be rewarded by enough wins to keep her support.

Some judges put up key people in kennel clubs, or known string-pullers. A string-puller is someone with influential friends in many clubs, and can arrange judging assignments almost at will.

Some judges put up the prettiest or sexiest-looking woman in the ring. It may be just the pleasure of small contacts, especially for older men judges who simply enjoy window shopping. The same may be said for older women judges and gay judges too, for that matter.

Some judges in Group competition place or ignore certain

breeds because of prejudices for or against the breed, regardless of the quality of the individual dogs.

Some judges may appear to punish an exhibitor by withholding deserved wins because of old grudges real or imagined.

All of these situations and more do come up, with some regularity. The stage is set for them; they are almost inevitable. Judges have absolute power within their rings. They may give or withhold whatever they want, and they may not be challenged or questioned. Although an exhibitor may ask for the judge's reason for a defeat, it must be done with the utmost deference or the judge can have the exhibitor disciplined.

Power corrupts and absolute power corrupts absolutely—if allowed to. Anyone in the position of dog show judge has within his gift the ability to give others what they most want—or to withhold it. And no one is allowed to challenge these whims.

Your objective then will be to steer your own little boat. Decide what you want out of the sport and what you're willing to do to get it. If you want to play the game honestly, you can, and you can be successful. Don't let anyone tell you you have to play dirty, because that is not true. The dirty players may seem to be the majority, but it's just because they get talked about more than the straight arrows. They make better gossip.

As your circle of friends in the dog fancy widens you'll find people in your breed, in every breed, who are survivors. They know the rules of the game, both the above-board set of rules and the realities behind the scenes. They accept the facts of dog show life and make the most of it. That's why they are survivors.

But they don't lower their own personal standards to play by what they perceive as common but wrong practices. They tend to their knitting, breed better and better dogs, smile when they win and smile when they lose, and carry on.

These are the dog show people who are worth knowing. The rest of them can go play their games. You don't need them.

10

People Problems

WHILE WE'RE ON THE SUBJECT of dogfolk in all their glory, let's take a minute to ponder the dangers inherent in the relationships ahead.

Dog people are no better, no worse, than humanity in general, in fact we're probably a pretty representative cross section. Because of the intensity of our feelings about our dogs, however, it's harder for us to keep an even stance emotionally.

You Win a Few, You Lose a Few

Friendships bloom overnight; someone speaks kindly of the dog we adore, and that's all it takes.

Hostilities also bloom overnight; someone tells us in condescending tones that our dog is a nice pet but has no business in the show ring. Again, that's all it takes.

This is not something we can shrug off, although we may pretend to make light of it. Our dogs *are* us, we are them. Love me, love my dog was not written in vain. We can be hurt by a remark so

If you can avoid jealousy, your best friends may be found among people in your own breed. Show weekends can be great times for exchanging news, gossip, and helpful information.

casual the speaker didn't even think of it as a put-down. And we never forget! Small slights and insults to our dogs live on in memory evergreen, and we'll spend the next two or three decades looking for a way to get even.

Friendships sometimes become wars of possession. You are *my* friend, and I don't want you to have any other friends but me. And if a third party comes along and I think you're starting to like her better than you like me, I'm going to look for ways to snip and snipe at her, make fun of her, belittle her dog. Childish, you say? Of course.

And it happens, all the time.

Some dogfolk have full and rewarding lives outside of the dog world. Others don't, so their dog show friends constitute their entire expanded family, support structure, call it what you will. It's not to be laughed at, because it is of genuine importance to these people.

Ego-feeding, hunger for belonging, being part of the pack, having someone to talk to—all of these crucial aspects of human life are being met by the kennel club gang, or the circle of friends and acquaintances that are seen weekend after weekend at the shows.

In some cases these are married women and men whose marriages aren't giving them what they need. In some cases they are single, divorced, gay and attached, gay and unattached, you name it. Dog friends become the most important human element of their lives. That being so, friendships can often become intense, even possessive.

I've known a number of women who have left marriages in order to set up housekeeping with another woman dog-buddy. These were not lesbian relationships, just a need for a partner who shared the passion for dogs and dog shows.

Friendships are fine. They're great if they don't overheat and explode. It's the enmities that will probably cause you problems.

You can create an enemy by buying your dog from someone Enemy has an old grudge against, or simply by not buying from Enemy although she had puppies when you were looking for one. She prizes her reputation as a breeder, so the fact that you went elsewhere is a slight but memorable slap in her face, unintentional though it might have been.

You can create an enemy by taking up a friendship with someone Enemy doesn't like, although that situation is more likely to end in a tug of war, with you as rope and prize.

You can create an enemy by buying a dog from her, then not winning with it, or telling the world about its faulty front, or putting it out with a handler that Enemy has a running feud with, or . . . well, the list is endless.

The Grapevine

Another fact of life with dogfolk that may seem dismaying at first is the grapevine. The smaller the breed numerically, the better the grapevine. Everyone knows everything about everyone, and it doesn't take long! By ten o'clock on Sunday night, an hour after people have arrived home from their shows, everyone on the grapevine knows who won what where, and who pulled his entry deliberately to break the major that would have finished somebody's dog, and what judges dumped what Specials in the Group.

Of course it's not just show wins that get talked about, it's everything. So and so just did another breeding with such and such a bitch, wasn't that twice in a row she bred that bitch? She's going to breed the insides right out of that poor animal. Or, somebody just heard that somebody sold a pet puppy to somebody and it's turned up with a bad genetic problem that that breeder claimed she never had in her line.

Once I mentioned in a letter, to a friend in New York, that I'd decided to neuter my old foundation sire. I had better sons and grandsons coming up, didn't need the old boy any more for breeding, but wanted to keep him because he was my special buddy, and I was still doing Obedience and Agility with him. Neutering would simplify logistics when bitches were in season.

Within two days came a phone call from Florida, from an acquaintance obviously trolling for gossip. She was all atwitter, having heard that I'd neutered Old Blue, and said the whole East Coast was up in arms about it, because he'd sired dogs in that area and the story was that he was siring blind puppies somewhere and that was why I neutered him.

This was not the first attack against Blue. The first came from a woman with an ongoing grudge against the man I'd bought the dog

116

from. She told someone who was buying a Blue daughter that it would be wise to stay away from that bloodline because of (hushed tones) the epilepsy problem. The receiver of this bit of business was an old hand at this game, and insisted on facts. Not innuendo. Please give me the names of epileptic dogs in any way related to Blue, she insisted, and she kept it up until the innuendo-passer finally had to back down.

My breed has a serious, widespread genetic problem, usually fatal. At the time of this writing, only two identified noncarriers exist in this country, one of which is my bitch Twink. I had taken her through the long, expensive test-breeding process and she proved out as a noncarrier, but meanwhile a rival, who desperately wanted to be the first to have a noncarrier, had also test-bred a dog that, unfortunately, did not prove to be a noncarrier.

A year or so later I received a phone call from a woman in Ohio, saying she had terrible news for me. She had just heard that one of Twink's daughters from her test litter had just died of the disorder in North Carolina. The story going around was that I had sold the dog with a faked medical record showing her to be normal when I knew her to be affected, and that this of course disproved my claim that Twink was a noncarrier.

I smelled a rat. There had been only one daughter from the test litter, alive and well in western Canada, not North Carolina. I was seething, as you can imagine, but did nothing. I could do nothing. The Ohio go-between refused to give me the name or phone number of the North Carolina dead-dog owner. In the end, the facts did surface. The story had been started by the same person who had claimed epilepsy for Old Blue. The dead dog in North Carolina did exist, but was connected to me only by the fact that her dam had previously been bred to Old Blue before I'd bought him.

Smear campaigns abound. Watch out for them.

The gossip grapevines will always exist and they do serve a purpose. It can be advantageous to know what's going on, who is bringing out a hot, new puppy, who is planning to special the old winner one more season, and so forth. There's no use telling you not to get drawn into gossiping. We all do it. It's fun. It's sometimes inaccurate, sometimes downright vicious, but watch out for anyone who takes a holier-than-thou stance and says "I never gossip."

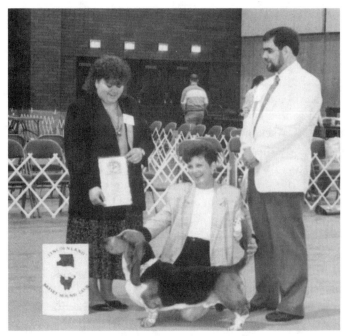

Winning may not be everything, but it sure does FEEL GOOD.

Orange cones in the parking area are commonly used by many dog exhibitors. These devices are designed to drive you mad as you head toward what looks like the last available parking place, to find it reserved by a row of cones.

Everyone does it. Everyone enjoys it. As long as it's just passing news items around, there's no harm in it, and maybe some good. It's our way of keeping in touch, of being interested in the others in our breed. We can only get that news from the dog friends who went showing this weekend.

It's when gossip is manufactured or distorted to be used as bullets in someone's shooting war that we find ourselves drawn into ugly situations. Sometimes we discover too late that we've been used to pass on hurtful lies. That's a terrible feeling.

Bucking the Busybodies

The key, if there is one, is to learn to recognize the poison peddlers in your breed, and to stay away from them. Every breed has them. They are liars, they are usually bitter, unhappy people who need to spoil it for others. They have no friends; they can't stand to see the friendships around them, and feel a continual need to sabotage good feelings among people.

If you find yourself wooed by one of these people, and you know she is a trouble maker, gently but firmly disengage yourself. If you've joined a dog club that seems unpleasantly roiling with animosities, quit. Find another, more peaceable group. Specialty clubs are particularly bad about warring factions, probably because there is so much direct competition between the breeder-exhibitors in the club.

An old rule of thumb, unfortunately true in too many cases, is that you'll find your best dog-buddies outside your own breed.

In dealing with nasty gossip and smear campaigns, the best advice is the hardest to follow: be above it. Don't pass on injurious news items if you don't know that they're true. Don't try to take an eye for an eye.

If you're being lied about, counter with the truth as calmly as you can, and then drop it. If you shoot back with palpable animosity, your audience will tend to write it off as a bitch-fight, both parties equally in the wrong. You lose as much credibility as if you fired the first shot.

Write down the following statement and put it on your refrigerator with a magnet: *We all end up with the reputations we deserve.*

Polishing Your Profile

As you carve your niche in the dog world, you will develop the reputation you deserve. We all do. Dogfolk may be inclined to enjoy a spicy bit of gossip, but most do have the ability to see through the motives behind it.

If you are pugilistic in your approach, always spoiling for a fight, always offering your chip-laden shoulder, you'll be perceived that way and you'll get to be a bore.

If you lie routinely, rest assured the people around you will pick up on it, will dislike you for it, and will cease to believe anything you say.

If you are a chameleon, this too will become obvious early on. People compare notes. You told A that she had a lovely dog, you really liked him, and you might want to breed to him some day. Then you told B that A's dog sucked pond scum and was garbage in comparison to B's superior animal. You think you're making them both happy, but surprise surprise, A and B start comparing their conversations with you, and you are hoist by your own petard.

Honesty is the best policy. Well, honesty mixed with a lot of reticence. Find something nice that you can honestly say about A's dog, but don't go any further than you have to, and don't discuss A's dog with B, or vice versa. Derogatory comments about a dog almost always find their way back to the dog's owner, and presto. Another enemy has been made!

You create your own reputation with every move you make. If you are straightforward in your dealings with people, honest and tactful in your speech, if you win and lose honestly and gracefully, you will be liked. And if you are liked, then smear campaigns, should they be aimed at you or your dog, will do more harm to the mud-slinger than to you.

Be above it.

11

Evaluating Your Dog

UNTIL YOU CAN do a decent job of evaluating your dog and the competition, you're going to be at the mercy of, well, of everyone.

The breeder you bought him from can insist he's a flawless dog and you're losing because of politics or your own bad handling.

A competitor can murmur sympathetically about this or that fault and you won't know if he's giving you an unwelcome fact or a mind job.

A judge can place him below what appears to be an obviously worse one, and you won't have a clue. Was it really a better dog, was yours a whole lot worse than you thought . . . or was the judge following his own best interests instead of judging dogs?

In short, you're going to feel helpless and disadvantaged as long as you have to depend on other people for opinions about your dog, and while you feel that way you're not going to be enjoying dog shows to the fullest.

So let's see if we can work in a little crash course here.

No Dog Is Perfect

The first thing you need to do is learn your breed's standard. Read it and study it until you pretty much know it by heart. It won't help a lot in evaluating, but it's the base that you need to build on.

I once got into an argument with a woman who swore her Maltese was a Bichon Frise and by George she had the registration papers to prove it. The dog had come from a puppy mill that raised both Maltese and Bichons and obviously somebody had grabbed the wrong fuzzy white puppy from the pen. But the woman argued on the basis of the breed standards' descriptions, and when I went to my AKC book to fuel my arguments, she was right. The descriptions were so vague in both standards that the little dog might have fit one breed just as well as the other.

So don't depend on just learning the standard to make an expert out of you. Your standard may say things like "head not too wide or too narrow." Big help. Some breed clubs provide illustrated standards, though, and these can be a considerable help.

Don't expect instant expertise. It takes years of studying one breed before the eye is honed. You can speed the process by continual practice. When you go to dog shows, go early and stay late, and watch the judging from ringside. Practice spotting the fine-boned and heavy-boned dogs in the class, or the shortest neck, or the lowest tail set.

Invest in a good book on dog structure and movement and study it, then practice your ringside judging again, this time from a position at the end of the diagonal mat, where the front and rear movement can be clearly seen.

Go through back issues of your breed's magazine and study the photos, again testing yourself. Why does that one look funny? Is the body too long?

Take this part of your hobby very seriously, and give yourself a semester of study, review, and testing. Ask questions of anybody whose judgment you value. At your club's conformation classes, ask other members to show you their dogs' faults so you can learn. Most will be happy to help if you are sincerely trying to learn.

Here are a few terms:

Heads

A dog's head might be faulted as being cheeky, skully, throaty, snipey, bitchy, or doggy. Cheeky means too full and sort of lumpy on the sides of the head, behind the jaws, where there's been maybe too much muscle development and the dog looks like he's packing walnuts for the winter. Skully can mean a prominent bumpy back-skull, top or sides or both. There's a ridge of bone arching backward from eye to ear, called the malar. In many breeds it's supposed to be as flat as possible, and if it arches or bulges outward it gives an ugly "skully" look to the dog's head. Throaty is just too much flesh on the underside of the dog's neck.

Snipey muzzles are too narrow, too shallow, too receding-chinnish to fit the rest of the dog. They might also be too short or too long. Usually they lack "fill before the eyes," that is, the planes appear to cave in from the eyes forward toward the nose so the foreface looks slightly concave where it should be convex, and often seems bony, veiny, and just all-over weak and unattractive.

Bitchy and doggy mean feminine and masculine, respectively. That one was easy, wasn't it? A bitchy male is unattractively re-fined, with perhaps a smallish head for the size of his body, a narrow snipey head—in short, a head that would look more appropriate on a bitch than on a dog. A doggy bitch, then, would be one who is too heavy-headed, too masculine.

Necks

People deplore short necks and admire long ones, but often the difference is not in the actual length of the neck but in the placement of the shoulders. If the shoulders slope back at a nice angle then the withers, which is the top of the shoulder blades, will lie a little farther back than they would if the shoulder blades were upright. It stands to reason. Upright shoulders make for a forward position of the withers, and this in turn adds visual length to the body and subtracts the same amount of visual length from the neck. These are steep shoulders, and bad news in most breeds.

If the shoulders lie well back, the neck appears to rise gracefully out of them at an upward angle before arching forward to the head. If the shoulders are straight up and down, the neck will seem to be coming out of the shoulders at a forward instead of upward angle, and then it has to bend itself sharply upward, often meeting the head at an unattractive angle. This is called a ewe-neck because it looks like that of a sheep.

Toplines

Toplines are more or less flat in most breeds, and arched in others. With flat toplines the most common fault is softness, or a back that tends to sag in the middle. Often they look fine while the dog is standing, possibly because the handler has his thumb strategically placed or has trained the dog to stand so as to make up for it. But when the dog starts to move, all is revealed, and the topline looks like the ole gray mare being less than what she used to be.

Arched, or roached, toplines usually crest a little to the rear of center, about over the loin area, though this may vary a little from breed to breed. If the apex is too far forward it's called a wheel back, and the dog probably moves badly.

People talk about tails being set on too high or too low, but of course the tail isn't set on at all; it's part of the spine, not a separate component like ears. If it appears too high or low it's usually because the pelvic girdle is at too flat or too steep an angle, or because of too much or too little flesh above the root of the tail. A tail set too low or too high can destroy the shape of the dog in outline.

Rib Spring

Rib spring refers to the amount of outward curve there is to the tops of the ribs coming out of the spine. Lots of rib spring gives a rounded body. Too little gives a flat-sided body. Some breeders in their quest for elegance produce dogs that look like highway fatalities, with bodies so flat and narrow they have to stand twice to cast a shadow. Not much room in there for hearts or lungs.

A dog whose body arches upward along its bottom line, from elbows to flanks, when it should go straight across, is described as herring-gutted, in reference to an old English artist who painted horses shaped that way.

124

Fronts

Years ago when I went to a famous Bedlington kennel to buy my first show Bedlington, the breeder stood the puppy up on the grooming table, motioned to the general area of his chest, and exclaimed, "Look at that front. Isn't that fantastic?" "Yeah, wow, fantastic," I agreed, having no idea at all what he was talking about. The chest? The front legs? The head?

I should have asked him to explain specifically what he meant, and I would have learned something, but I was nineteen and couldn't admit that I didn't already know it all.

"Front" generally means the whole front assembly of chest, shoulders and forelegs. The Bedlington breeder meant that the shoulders had good layback, the chest was well developed rather than caving inward between the forward points of the shoulders, and the front legs were parallel to each other, neither too close nor too far apart, with the elbow neatly aligned close to the rib cage, not flopping loosely to the sides. And the feet aimed straight forward rather than outward like those of a ballet dancer.

A narrow front means lack of rib spring and body width, and usually goes with feet toeing out, to keep the dog from tipping over like a pedestal table. A wide front means too much chest between the forelegs.

A fiddle front is one with forelegs too wide at the top, and with leg bones that curve inward as they go down, usually ending in feet that point outward again for balance. Curved lines may be the artist's delight, but you don't want them on your dog's front unless your breed calls for it.

Suppose your puppy toes out at four months of age, but your breeder insists it's temporary and he'll grow out of it. Run your hands down the legs and see if the long leg bones feel straight to you, or whether they seem to bend or curve inward on the way down. If the bones feel straight, chances are the toeing out is just compensation for the narrow body, for balance, and the narrow body may well be just a puppy stage. So there's a good chance that the toeing out will correct later on as the chest widens and the whole leg moves outward. But if the bone itself is curving, chances are that's going to be permanent.

125

Rears

Hind legs might be cowhocked, straight stifled, too close, too wide, bowlegged or sickle-hocked. It's a nice selection of things to worry about back here.

Cowhocks are maybe the most common rear fault, and sometimes they are just a puppy stage that corrects with maturity, but don't count on it. Looking at the dog from the rear, the hind legs should make a straight line from hip to floor, with all the leg bones aligned in an unbending column. This is important because it's this column of bone that supports the dog's weight and propels it forward when he moves. If that line of support zigzags from side to side, angling outward hips to stifle, then inward stifle to hock, and outward again hock to foot, it is weak because at each of those corners there are hinges where there shouldn't be, and all his life, every step that dog takes puts a little pressure, a little stretch, on tendons and ligaments that weren't meant to be pulled in that direction.

That's cowhocks. Stand behind a cow some time and you'll see the likeness. In extreme cases the dog's hind legs, viewed from the rear, look like the letter *X,* angling toward each other in the middle, or hocks, and outward again from hocks down. In milder cases the column of leg bones is angled just a little and it might be hard to spot, especially if you're looking through a pile of coat. But if you stand behind the dog, wrap your hands around his hind legs and run them downward, you'll feel the outward angle of the bones from hock to floor.

Clever grooming in coated breeds can do much to give the illusion of straight legs, but a good judge will find the flaw, especially when the dog moves.

Bowlegged is the opposite of cowhocked, with legs curving away from each other at the hocks, rather than toward each other. It's just as bad a fault, though probably less common.

Straight stifles are legs that are too straight up and down when you look from the side. There's not enough bend at the stifle and hock joints because the bone isn't long enough, so the hind leg is almost straight up and down. This gives a short stride and a rough, bouncy look to the topline when the dog is in motion. The opposite

126

fault is overangulation, too much bend. Rear angulation impresses judges even when it's wrong for the breed, and some breeds have been ruined by competitive breeders going for the maximum and ending up with dogs who can barely get out of their own way.

The more angulation in the rear, the longer the dog's stride will be, hence the more power and speed he'll generate. But the front end had better have matching angulation in the shoulder layback, or the front legs will be taking shorter steps than the back ones. This usually results in sidewinding, where the rear is moving off to the side of the front of the dog. Also known as "crabbing," it is a bad movement fault in the show ring. Sometimes sidewinding is just puppy silliness, but if it persists, the dog may not have balanced angulation front to rear, and is compensating by swinging sideways.

Sickle hocks are legs that angle forward, hock to ground, when viewed from the side. The leg should be perpendicular to the ground from the hock down. If it's bent forward it's a weak support, a weak working joint, and usually causes a sort of feeble paddling gait in the rear, with no propulsive power.

The rear is the dog's engine. It's the source of the power that propels him forward. If the hind legs are weakly constructed he'll be hitting on four cylinders instead of eight, and he'll run out of gas. It takes a lot more energy to propel a fifty-pound dog forward on sickle hocks, bowlegs, cowhocks or straight stifles than it does with sound running gear, perpendicular hocks that can push off against the ground and thrust forward.

Good judges are picky about rear soundness, and rightly so.

More on Movement

Some other common movement faults are weaving and paddling, pacing, moving too close or too wide, lack of reach or drive, lateral toss—the list goes on but these are enough to start with. These are the most common.

I know someone who is fond of saying that a certain dog moves like a dream. For years I watched him saying it about dogs that were hopping, sidewinding, pacing or paddling. To him they moved like a dream, especially if they went fast while hopping, sidewinding, pacing and paddling. Finally I realized he just liked to watch dogs zipping around show rings.

Some exhibitors and an unfortunate number of judges also seem to think that if a dog is going fast with lots of hair blowing around him he's sure a mover, by George. But if you want to get anywhere in dogdom you'll have to develop a more discerning eye than that, for movement faults.

Weaving, paddling and braiding, are interchangeable or at least confusingly close terms for front legs that do funny things. Paddling is when the front feet are tossing out to the side with every step, when viewed head-on. Often the elbows shift loosely out of alignment at the same time, out away from the body, so the whole picture is similar to cowhocks, only in front. Weaving or braiding is when the forelegs move so close to each other that they have to swing out to the side with every step in order to get around each other. This happens in the rear, too, sometimes, when a dog moves so close behind that his legs do a little sideways swing to get around each other.

A dog might be weaving and paddling, both. It looks awful, and it's pretty hard to win with a dog that moves that way, on either end.

Pacing is when both legs on the same side of the dog are moving forward at the same time. It's a lateral gait as opposed to the trot, which is diagonal, and correct. It's diagonal in that the right front is moving forward at the same time as the left rear, and vice versa. In the lateral pace, right rear and right front move together. Pacing is an easier gait for a tired dog to use, and sometimes dogs that are built wrong, cowhocked or whatever, tend to pace in the show ring because their muscles are too tired to sustain a trot. Sometimes a sharp snap of the lead can pop a dog out of his pacing. Sometimes not.

Pacing is a sure way to the end of the line in the show ring.

Lateral toss is the sway of the hips from side to side, seen from the rear as the dog trots. It usually means that his hind legs are hitting too wide, the feet hitting the floor several inches apart instead of close together, so he is, in effect, tossing himself from side to side with every step. It's wasted motion, it looks bad, and good judges will spot it as you gait away from them on the diagonal. In some breeds with short legs and broad bodies, it is unavoidable and therefore correct.

Lack of drive refers to length of stride being too short to propel the dog forward. Straight stifles, sickle hocks, cowhocks or any combination of these can contribute to lack of drive. Not all judges spot it but the better ones do.

As a general rule, the best movement is that which produces the most forward propulsion with the least wasted energy. Engrave that in your memory and it will simplify the job of judging movement.

Side movement, which just means movement as viewed from the side, should be smooth-looking, with minimum bounce of the topline and with long, smooth strides. Short, choppy strides and trampoline tops both show wasted up-and-down motion, wasted because it's not propelling the dog forward.

Front movement, viewed with the dog coming toward you, should be neat-looking, with the feet moving inward toward the center of the body as speed increases, to prevent lateral toss, or sideways sway. Elbows should move closely against the body, not angling out. Toes should be coming straight forward, not east-westing like a ballet dancer.

Rear movement, viewed going away, should be much the same, minimal sideways toss of the rear, and the leg bones in a straight line hip to floor, for maximum support. This straight line should angle inward toward center as speed increases.

Balance

The most important single aspect of a dog may be the one that is hardest to learn, but the one most valued by good judges—balance. When you can spot a beautifully balanced dog and understand that *that's* what looks so good about him, you'll be well on your way to having an eye for dogs.

Balance means all the parts being in perfect proportion to each other so the dog looks all of a piece, and just right. The total is more than the sum of the parts.

If a dog has a rather short head, with a comparably short neck, body and running gear, he'll be classified as cobby but he'll look good. If a dog is long and lean in all those areas he's a racy type, but again, he looks good.

But if he's got a short head, short neck, long body, long tail, short forelegs and long hind legs, well, you get the picture and it's not pretty.

It's quite possible to have a dog with no actual faults, nothing you can put a finger on, and yet he just doesn't strike your eye. He repels you but you're not sure why. It might be that his owner has just insulted your dog so you're looking for faults in his, or it might be that his dog is not well balanced. A skully head with a snipey muzzle. Straight front assembly with overangulated rear. Shallow, shelly body with thickly muscled neck.

A beautifully balanced dog is likely to out-win one that is superior in this or that particular but lacks overall cohesion.

This is just an overview, not intended to be an in-depth lesson in structure, movement or judging. There are some excellent books available that go into those subjects in great detail. But do put some effort into educating your eye. You'll be surprised at things you can spot about dogs a year from now that you can't see now.

Some people never develop an eye for dogs no matter how hard they work at it, and others have a natural eye. Most of us fall somewhere in between, with eyes capable of learning the fine points in our breed, and later in other breeds.

Unless you plan to coast through life as a perennial novice in the dog world, you'd better do your homework. You don't want to be like the breeder who, after ten years in the sport, still thought "ewe-necked" meant a neck shaped like the letter *U*.

12

Losers Weepers

THERE IS NOTHING more disheartening to a new exhibitor than having to drive home from the shows week after week, disappointed and confused. Your good dog just lost—again. After a while you become disappointed, confused, and angry. Then you become discouraged, cynical, and that's when you decide you've had enough.

Much of this angst could be avoided if only we knew *why* we lost. Then, if it's something within our power to change, we can change it. If not, we can try to avoid repeating it.

Often it's not just the loss that depresses us, it's not understanding it that drives us nuts. And sometimes there is no understandable reason behind it. The judge may simply have not known which dog to point the fateful finger at, and ended up eenie-meenie-miney-moing his way out of his quandary.

Let's spend a moment in quiet meditation over some of the most common reasons for being passed over by the fateful finger.

Be Honest About Your Dog

Your dog isn't good enough. Few beginners are lucky enough to buy a top-quality show prospect on their first try. Dogs that good don't come along very often, and when they do, they're seldom sold to new exhibitors, if they're sold at all. The top breeders, producing the top dogs, are astute enough to spot the outstanding youngsters and to hang on to them or sell them where their show potential will be realized. Few newcomers can do justice to a top dog.

Sometimes, of course, a really good dog is born to a novice breeder and sold to a novice exhibitor who may or may not know what he's got. It's everybody's dream that this will happen, and it happens occasionally, but don't count on its happening to you. Most new dog people start with something less than a top-drawer specimen, and do their learning with that dog. Then later, when they've developed an eye for the breed and a few personal connections with good breeders, they can move up to a better show animal.

Meanwhile, you're back in the show ring with the medium-quality starter pup. Your dog may be in the "nice" category, basically show quality, good enough to pick up a few wins here and there, but just not outstanding. He is not good enough to get most of the wins most of the time. He may be a notch or two lower than that on the scale, and barely classify as show quality.

It will be hard for you to know for sure about this until you've been in dogs long enough to have developed your own ability to assess your breed. Until then you have to depend on what other people are telling you about your dog, and you can't always be sure they know what they're talking about.

To further muddy the view, we have the old bugaboo of kennel blindness, a visual defect endemic to dogfolk, in which we cannot see faults in our own dogs, but see them with perfect clarity in others. You might study structure and movement till the cowhocks come home and still not be able to see it in your own dog.

Here's a trick to foil kennel blindness. When you look at your dog, pretend he belongs to someone you hate, and you're trying to find something to criticize him for when you gossip spitefully about his rotten owner.

*   *   *

Your dog is good enough but someone has a better one. If that's the case, then time will take care of the problem. From time to time in any breed an unusually good one comes along and cleans up, show after show. If you've gotten yourself stuck behind one like that, just bide your time and the dog will finish its championship and retire or move up to specials, and get out of your hair. Meanwhile, you might try to find weekends with more than one set of shows, figure out which one the big winner is likely to be at, and go the other direction. The *Show Awards* section of the *Gazette* can help you do some research on which judges have been putting up that dog, and this may help you to figure out which show he'll be entered in. You can check to see which shows he was entered in this time last year, since most of us tend to go to the same shows every year.

If you're being beaten week after week by the same dog and it's a good one, then swallow your lumps and accept it gracefully. The world is wagging as it should, even though for the moment you're not getting what you want. A few years from now you may be the one with the big winner, and you'll want to be admired by the people you're beating, not hated.

How's Your Grooming?

If you honestly feel your dog is as good as the ones who are beating him, then take a hard look at your presentation. If yours is a coated breed, does he have as much coat as the competition or are you making excuses for sparse belly coat and scraggly leg furnishings? Be honest now. You may have fallen into the habit of making excuses for the state of his coat but you can't expect the judge to do the same.

If it's a matter of grooming, then the ball is in your court. It's up to you to find out what other people are doing to make their dogs whiter or fluffier or shinier than yours. And do it. Ask around. Don't ask your competitors but find someone you trust in your breed or in another breed with a similar coat type, and pick their brains. Experiment at home. Use shampoos with bluing in them. Use coat dressings, power dryer, sprays—whatever the majority of people in your breed are using on their dogs.

How illegal is foreign stuff in the coat? That's a matter of viewpoint. AKC says anything that changes a dog's appearance in the ring is illegal. At the same time, the coat and color enhancers are sold at every vendor booth at every dog show, quite openly.

What do most judges think about it? As far as I can tell most judges expect you to come into the ring with a professionally presented dog. White should be white, colors should be bright, and if it doesn't actually come off on their hands, they approve. Many judges used to be handlers, and as handlers they knew all the tricks of the trade and practiced them, too. A few judges are sticklers and will excuse dogs from the ring for excessive chalking, and that's as it should be. But for the most part, do what you need to do to make your dog look like the others being shown in your breed in your area.

But do practice at home. If you're going to start chalking your dog, do full-dress rehearsals at home until you feel confident that you can do a good, subtle job of whitening, so that your dog looks bright and clean and isn't going to send up chalk clouds when the judge pats him.

And if you do use chalk or sprays, be sure to bathe your dog as soon as you get home from the show. Leftover "daffy" in the coat will break it off and may cause skin irritations.

Your problem might be an unnoticed clump of coat around the dog's hocks. It looks okay to you on the grooming table at home, but when he moves, it flops to the inside and makes him look cowhocked. Or it might be a little extra hair on the outside of the elbow; again, it looks fine on the table but makes him look out at the elbow when he moves. Or it might be some extra fluff over his croup making him look high in the rear.

How's Your Handling?

If your dog and your grooming are up to speed, then maybe the problem is your handling. If you have access to a camcorder, have a friend videotape you next time you're in the ring, and study the tape carefully. Is your right arm waving in the breeze as you gait? Is your body bent like a pretzel, down and around in front of your dog's face? Do you look like Raggedy Ann dumped in a heap when

134

you kneel to stack your dog on the floor? Does it take you too many quivering minutes to stack your dog on the table?

Are you posing your dog by grabbing both his hind legs and jerking them into place instead of picking up the hock and neatly setting the leg straight while supporting the dog's weight so he's not panicking? Are you taking forever with the front legs when all you needed to do was to set the far one to match the near one, picking it up at the elbow rather than way down low where it scares the dog by throwing him off-balance?

By doing all this nervous novice stuff you're telling the judge that you're new at this, you're scared witless and therefore your dog isn't much good or you'd be used to winning instead of obviously expecting the ax.

When you come into the ring, is your face frozen in terror, a death mask with staring eyes and disengaged brain? Or do you sail in smiling confidently, eager to show this lucky judge your wonderful dog that you've been saving as a surprise to brighten the lucky judge's day?

A smile can be a whole lot more than an umbrella. It sends a message to the judge that you're happy to be in his ring, with this good dog at your side, and you can hardly wait for the nice win he's about to give you.

You'd be surprised how well this works.

If you look stiff and scared and miserable, you send all kinds of subliminal messages to the judge. You don't think your dog has a hope in hell. You wish it was over and you could escape. You live in terror of judges in general and this one in particular.

Even though he is primarily focused on your dog, your face is in his peripheral view, and when he's telling you to take them all around together please, he's looking right at you. What you transmit from your facial expression he will receive, consciously or otherwise.

You and your dog may look like gangbusters, but you still might be blowing it in ways you're not aware of. I showed a flashy young dog to a string of good wins, then began losing when I didn't think I should have. One day after I gaited him down and back the judge said, "Take him again slower, he's doing something funny in the rear." I gaited him again at walking speed instead of running, and she nodded and gave him the win.

It doesn't happen often, but the dream is not impossible: this owner handler, waiting to compete in the Non-Sporting Group, later guided her French Bulldog to Best in Show.

A friend and I took him out to the parking lot and I had her gait him away from me at three distinct speeds, slow, medium, and fast. At slow and fast he spraddled in back, hitting wide and lateral-tossing all over the place. At a moderate trot, he was fine.

I'd gotten so carried away with the joy of showing this self-assured little dog I'd started gaiting him faster and faster, and didn't realize I was blowing myself out of the ribbons.

Since then my friends and I make a point of gaiting each other's new dogs at various speeds, at training class, and memorizing the exact speed that's best for each one.

Another friend had a dog who hit a losing streak when he began resetting his forelegs, way too far apart, while she was setting his rear. She'd already stacked his front, assumed it was fine, and didn't realize he was standing there looking like a Mack truck in front, smiling and wagging his tail and looking awful.

Some dogs with sound hocks make themselves look bad by pulling in their hocks when they are stacked on the judging table. It's the insecurity of the table, not structural flaws, but the judge may not have time to figure that out. Some dogs clench up through the shoulders for the same reason, making themselves look steep-shouldered and rough through the withers, when a more relaxed stance would settle things nicely into place.

A common mistake beginners make is stretching their dogs out too much, so the forelegs are angled forward rather than straight down. It causes a dip in the topline and a general hobbyhorse look, sometimes called posting.

Some dogs post themselves, rocking backward after they're stacked, pulling away from something you are doing, like gripping them painfully around the muzzle and pinching lips against teeth. Gentle stroking under the throat may bring them forward again, or a pull of the tail.

A videotape or snapshot of your dog in the ring, in a lineup with the rest of the class, might show that he isn't stacked quite as sharply as the others. He might be standing in a rather ordinary-looking position while the others are stretched out till their toplines look like ski slopes and their necks look a mile long. Don't expect a judge working on a tight schedule to go looking for hidden gold in your dog. If yours is the one in the class of five that looks dumpy on that last glance down the line, tough luck.

When you're starting out as a new exhibitor, of course you are going to make all these mistakes. You will look scared because you will be scared. Your face won't radiate confidence because you can't dredge any up and you're too focused on your lead and your dog and your feet and a dozen other details to have any mental energy left for faking facial expressions.

Not to worry. It all comes with experience. Just don't be downhearted at the defeats along the way, at least some of which you're probably generating yourself by looking and acting like the beginner you are. Hang in there. It gets better.

Hidden Causes

If you and your dog are genuinely good enough, and you're beginning to get your share of attention some of the time, but are still crashing up against unexplained defeats, the answer may lie out of sight.

It may be that the judge has a personal connection, unknown to you, with the exhibitor he just put up over you. Miss Elkhound may have just been talking with him about the Nonesuch judging assignment. Or he might have run across the other handler last night in the coffee shop at the hotel and gotten his arm twisted.

Possibly, the handler who beat you just mailed the judge a copy of a win picture from a show last month, and her face is fresh in his mind.

She may be the club member who gave him a lift from the airport or the hotel or yesterday's show and made friends with him at that time.

Possibly, the judge doesn't know her at all but he has a warm spot for her because she has curly red hair and freckles just like his high school sweetheart whom he's never gotten over.

Of course, things like this shouldn't enter into dog judging but judges are human and are as subject to their subconscious as the rest of us. We all have had the experience of inexplicable instant likes or dislikes when meeting new people. They remind us on some level of an important person in our past, and the impact, good or bad, carries over to the present.

A more common situation, though, is the familiar face factor. Judges tend to put up people they've seen before a little more frequently than total strangers, even though there is no personal connection. If the familiar face consistently shows good dogs, judges often come to associate "familiar strangers" with quality animals and often act accordingly. On an average, a judge might do a particular breed two or three times a year, in a given state. So even if you're showing all the time, it takes a while for your face to start registering in the minds of judges. They see lots of faces at every show, every weekend, and since they are primarily focusing on the dogs, they might see one exhibitor half a dozen times before she starts imprinting on the memory and carrying over from one show to the next, several months hence.

So if a judge begins to think of you as a familiar face it means you've been doing a lot of showing over an extended period of time. That means you probably have good dogs or you wouldn't keep doing it. There is a correlation in most judges' minds between beginners and losers, fair or not. The average judge, faced with a close decision between two dogs of equal quality, will usually put up the experienced person he's most familiar with over the obvious novice. If the novice's dog is clearly better, this is unfair. If the two dogs are actually equal in quality, it's still unfair but somewhat understandable.

You too can become a familiar face. All it takes is years of constant showing, with good dogs well presented. It helps if you get an occasional win picture taken and use that opportunity to make a good impression on the judge. If you can exchange a bit of kidding with judges who like to break the monotony of the day that way, you have a better chance at being remembered. The absolute best way to be remembered is to show fine dogs in top condition and have them showing perfectly. Do that and you'll always be happy.

It also helps to expect the unexpected. The judge may like the other guy's dog for personal reasons. Once I was visiting a handler's kennel as he was unloading after a show trip. "Just got a four-point major on that bitch," he said, pointing to the dog in the exercise pen. Quite frankly, it was the ugliest bitch I'd ever seen. "Who was the judge?" I asked, trying not to wrinkle a lip. He named one of the best-known and most respected judges on the circuit.

With my usual tact I said, "That's the ugliest bitch I've ever seen. How did you pull it off?"

He laughed and said that he was astounded himself at the win, and asked the judge later whatever possessed him to put her up. Judge said, "Well, I've got one at home that looks just like her, and she's my pet and I love her, and nobody ever gave her a win, so that's why I put up your bitch."

It was, admittedly, dreadful judging, and a decision that must have sent every other exhibitor in the class home shaking his or her head in puzzlement and anger. No one ever knew why the obviously worst dog in the ring got the coveted major.

It may be that you walked into a political situation. A favor was being returned and you happened to be in the same class. In most of those cases no one can see the string-pulling that went on, other times and places. Happily, it happens less often than is widely supposed. It may simply be a matter of the judge's ignorance of your breed. This is the easiest and most frequent direction in which blame is flung, sometimes unfairly. Sometimes not. Some judges rushed through several breeds within their Group in order to get full-group approval, skimming over the study, learning what they needed to know to pass the tests, but in the same way school kids learn just enough to get the passing grade. A week later they've forgotten what square root means, and your judge has forgotten whether height is a disqualification in your breed or only a fault.

In a perfect world, every judge would be an in-depth expert on every breed, and he would line up his placements in every class in strict order of excellence. It's not a perfect world, folks. The reality we have to live with is that judges come in all levels of competence, from the very good to "who hired this turkey?"

There are judges who are very good in some breeds and out of their depth in others.

There are judges who are fixated on one point and will always put up the biggest, the hairiest, the fastest-moving, the most animated. This is almost always bad judging. I know of one judge who gave a Group first to a dog because it was the only dog in the lineup who looked toward the judge rather than staring at its handler's bait hand as the others were doing.

There are judges who are simply too old. One poor soul comes to mind and will of course remain nameless. He excused from the ring an entire class of American Water Spaniels, as being undersized and of terrible quality. He was confused and thought he was judging Irish Water Spaniels. I believe he was the same judge who excused an entire class of bitches for having no testicles, thinking he was on Open Dogs.

There was a Toy judge who angrily withheld the ribbon from a little girl's longcoat Chihuahua, scolding the child for the dog's lack of quality, when in fact it was a Papillon whose young handler had been herded erroneously into the ring by an overzealous steward.

There are judges who are careful about their first placements but don't make the same effort with second, third and fourth, just taking them in the order they stand, or shooting the fateful finger half cocked, so to speak. Or they may start the day being thorough and good but slack off when they get tired, thirsty, or sore-backed from standing all day on concrete and bending repeatedly to examine dogs.

Most judges sincerely try to find the best dog and put it up. If they are consistent in what they select as much as possible, they cannot be faulted.

Just as true, not all judges are good ones, though, and although it's irritating and frustrating to have to put up with bad judging, don't take these decisions as a reflection on your dog or your handling ability. If the judging is truly awful, make a note of it, and do not show under that one again. An entry is a vote of confidence and as such it's the exhibitor's only suffrage. If we used it more often we might be able to improve judging, and, by extension, the dog sport.

In the Long Run

But often we show under judges we don't respect, simply because they might put us up, we have dogs to get finished and it's a show we want to go to, so we accept Mr. Turkey and go anyhow, and when we do that we shouldn't feel too down in the dumps when we lose. We sort of asked for it.

If a judge is consistent in the type he prefers, even if I disagree, I might show under him with the right dog. If he always puts up little–cute dogs over rangy-elegant ones, then that's okay. I'll show him my next little–cute, but save my entry money on the rangies. If a judge has an obvious leaning toward young girls, young men, or whatever, I make note of it and enter or not as I see fit, knowing who else is likely to be at that show and figuring my odds accordingly.

Judges who follow no pattern, putting up one type one day and the opposite the next, are harder to figure. Entering under them seems to be a crapshoot, and I'll gamble my entry fees or not, depending on how much I want to go showing that weekend, or whether it might be a major entry and therefore worth the gamble.

You might have lost simply because, while your dog was no worse than the winner, it was no better either, and this time the luck fell in the other direction. That happens. If that's all it is, keep on truckin', your chance may come next weekend.

If your losing streak seems incurable and goes on for more than a year of reasonably steady showing, then it might be time to give up on that dog and keep him as a pet or find him a good home and go shopping for a better one. Out of all of the reasons I've listed here for losing, by far the most common is simply that the dog isn't good enough. Take heart. Most of us start out with dogs that aren't good enough, and most of us graduate to better dogs, better wins, better times. You can, too.

13

Are We Having Fun Yet?

IF NOT, is it our fault? Could be.

The enjoyment of the sport of showing dogs is pretty much in the mind. If you set out to have a good time win or lose, to enjoy a day at the dog show with old friends, new friends, beautiful dogs and fun stuff to buy at the booths, you're guaranteed a good time. If you set out bitching about the 4:00 A.M. reveille and the chore of loading and unloading and the rotten weather, if you're tied in knots inside with nervousness or fear of defeat, or if nothing short of a Group first will make the day worthwhile, then the day probably isn't going to be worthwhile.

For most of us starting out in dogs, all shows are exciting at first. We feel part of an intriguing and exhilarating world, there are endless things to learn, everyone is so nice to us and we really don't expect to win much of anything.

But the honeymoon doesn't last forever. Comes a time when the hours of preparation followed by the hours of driving don't seem sufficiently compensated by the five minutes in the ring and the third out of five placement under the judge we had high hopes for. Booth

One way to enhance your enjoyment of dog show trips is to supply yourself with maximum creature comfort. For me, this self-contained camper van was the answer. The topper allows stand-up comfort for in-the-van grooming, away from crowded grooming areas. The generator runs air-conditioner, heater, TV, lights, soft music, blow-dryer. Across the rear is a comfortable bed, where the dogs love to lie while at the shows. Along the driver-side is a homemade cabinet containing grooming table, dining table, stove, sink, kitchen storage, and other amenities. The exercise pens attach to the van side, so dogs can hop in and out easily and don't need to be walked in the wee hours. The van doubles as a practical and dependable everyday vehicle as well.

shopping isn't fun anymore; we already have a surfeit of cute T-shirts and bumper stickers. We're beginning to realize that dog show hot dogs are universally awful, and coffee with grooming chalk in it isn't cordon bleu.

We've done enough winning that the surprise is gone and expectation has set in. Third out of five is no longer winning, it's losing because we had hopes for the points and felt our dog was the best in the ring, paws down. We heard whispers that the exhibitor who won was staying at the judge's hotel last night and they were seen in the cocktail lounge and it all looked pretty fishy. We suspect dirty doings and we're furious.

And besides that, two weeks ago we dropped a disparaging remark to a friend about another friend's dog, and the remark was passed on and embellished and now those two former friends have cemented an alliance that excludes us. And we've just heard a lie about our dog, apparently started by those two and spread with malice aforethought.

Are we having fun?

Probably not.

It's at this point that the lasters are separated from the drop-outs.

The Nature of a Laster

The lasters keep showing, keep learning, keep studying their own dogs and others so that they know when they deserve the wins and the losses. If the loss was justified, okay, someone else had a better dog. If the loss wasn't justified, make notes in your judges notebook and avoid walking into the same situation a second time.

A laster is realistic about his dog and keeps enough emotional distance that he is able to move on to a better dog if the first one doesn't pan out. Total blind love for a mediocre dog causes endless grief to new exhibitors who have to swallow losses that they don't understand or accept week after week.

A laster works at the sport as any serious competitor does, whether amateur or professional. He puts in the years of club work and breeding and study, mistake making and lump taking. Eventually it pays off and the wins come rolling in.

A non-show doggy activity which gives great pleasure is working with 4-H youngsters. Here, young competitors for our county fair's Agility class work their dogs over
Touchwood's training course.

Are we having fun?
You bet your sweet life.

OTHER PATHS

Conformation showing isn't the only game in town. If after giving
it a good shot you decide it's just not for you, but you still love your
dog and dogs in general, and want the fun of doing *something* with
them, consider the options, any of which can be enjoyed along with
conformation showing, of course.

Obedience—In its early years the sport of obedience was often
considered a dumping ground for dogs not good enough to win in
conformation competition. Not true anymore, if it ever was. The
main difference is that obedience appeals to a slightly different
personality type than conformation. Obedience offers much more
control, for one thing. You can control the outcome, the score, by
working and practicing and polishing your dog's performance. In
conformation you're stuck with the dog you have and can only
enhance his winning potential to a limited degree.

In its early years obedience was considered a pass-fail sport,
with the emphasis on getting three passing scores and achieving
your dog's title. Competitors genuinely cheered each other on and
moaned over the broken sit-stay or the second-command recall. Any
score over 170 was a hugging event.

Things changed as the sport got more popular, more crowded,
more expert. AKC added a new title, Obedience Trial Champion,
which required winning classes and showing at the highest level for
long periods of time. Now I'd venture to say that things are every bit
as competitive and intense in obedience as in conformation, and the
cheating is just as pervasive and inventive. It's a different kind of
cheating, where wins aren't bought with assignments or money or
even the familiar face advantage, but with liver taped to the thigh
under the jeans.

While it is still possible to train a dog at home out of a book,
and go showing and eventually get his title, it's almost never done
that way anymore. Now, a good training class is a must, and if you
want to go for good scores, class placements and High in Trial

possibilities, it takes a good competitive-level instructor and at least a year's worth of daily workouts at home with your dog, continually polishing and perfecting every sit, every front and finish.

Training seminars are popular, weekend get-togethers with exhibitors and their dogs working with top instructors, usually people who have written currently popular training books. These seminars can be lots of fun, good chances to make friends and to learn a lot in a short span of time.

Your breed can be important in obedience. Some breeds have a natural affinity for obedience work. Some don't. A herding breed with generations of experience in following the shepherd's hand signals in moving the flock is a better bet than a terrier who was bred to work on its own, killing rats in the barn. Working and sporting breeds were developed for their ability to obey commands and accept the hunter or farmer as boss, while toy breeds were developed to be passive companions.

But these generalities are made a mockery of every day in the obedience ring, and that is fun! Doing well with a terrier is somehow more satisfying, to me, than the same score would have been with a Sheltie. There have been top obedience dogs in virtually every breed. If yours is a nontraditional obedience breed and you're drawn to the sport, go to it. Most instructors and judges enjoy the novelty of something different, and though the judges won't, or shouldn't, score breeds differently, they will respect you for doing a super job with a breed known for hardheaded independence.

When I show in obedience I try to play a personal-best game. I lack the patience to train my dogs to an ant's eyebrow before I jump into the ring, so I'm seldom in the ribbons. I set my goal at getting the title in as few shows as possible, and on improving my score from show to show. They may not be the scores serious obedience fans would brag about, but they satisfy me and keep my enjoyment level high.

Tracking—If obedience doesn't excite you, how about the somewhat obscure but wonderful world of tracking? Tracking tests aren't held in conjunction with dog shows because they require lots of space; therefore they tend to go unnoticed by the majority of dog

148

show people, but I find them the most purely enjoyable of all the doggy endeavors I've tried.

In a tracking test, a dog on a harness and very long lead follows a trail made by a walking person, finds a dropped article at the end, and that's it. The trail is about a quarter mile long, over fields and through weeds and brush. It's aged a half hour to two hours. It begins at a pair of marker flags, becomes invisible, and ends at a brown cotton work glove dropped in some mysterious spot three fields away.

This really is a pass-fail sport. If your dog follows the track and finds the glove and shows clearly that he has found it, he passes. If he gets too far off the track, the Whistle of Fate is blown and you're out, and everybody including the judge mourns with you. But if you pass, the judge cheers, and the gallery (made up of other competitors) cheers and genuinely means it, too, because your win takes nothing away from theirs. You win your tracking title. Sometimes the judge hugs you. Once a judge sent me a congratulations card after a tracking test. Once on a rainy, muddy day the judge got out of the back of the truck carrying three exhibitors to a distant starting point, and helped push the truck out of the mud along with the rest of us.

Tracking tests are usually limited to ten or twelve competitors, because each track takes so much time and space. The tests may be held in a scout camp, state park, possibly on private land. The tests I've gone to have included luscious big breakfasts for judges and competitors in the park shelter house, dogs at our feet, scrambled eggs and bacon aplenty. And usually there has been an equally good lunch, all food provided by the host club. There are trophies or award plaques for every passing dog, and picture-taking and fun, and a heartfelt joy in accomplishment.

As in obedience, every dog at a tracking test has been through hundreds of hours of training time at home, starting from square one and working until the skill was learned and solid. Then, to qualify to enter a tracking test, dog and handler had to find a tracking judge, set up a meeting with the judge, usually at the judge's home or somewhere nearby, and perform for the judge a complete official track. A passing performance on this qualifying test gives the dog the right to enter an official tracking test. The successful completion of one official test gives the dog his TD (Tracking Dog) degree, which is added at the end of his name.

There are three aspects of tracking that I love dearly. One is the outdoor exercise, tramping over the countryside doing my practice tracks two or three times a week. That's good, healthy exercise.

The second is the quality of genuine good sportsmanship in the sport. It's not that tracking enthusiasts are superior human beings; in fact, they are usually the same people who slug it out in conformation and obedience. Our better natures are allowed to surface in tracking, because there is no way to cheat in a tracking test, and because we are not in competition with each other. For those of us whose main loves are other areas of the dog world, tracking still provides a wonderful break from the negative aspects of competitive life.

As with obedience, any breed can do tracking; some will do it quite a bit better than others. The breeds who have the most difficulty are those with extremely foreshortened faces, and tiny dogs with very short legs for whom a quarter-mile trek through long grass would be herculean.

Agility—My other favorite when I need a sanity-break from conformation showing is Agility—a high-voltage activity developed in England in 1978. At the time of this writing the sport of Agility is still relatively new to dog enthusiasts in the United States. But it is a very appealing sport, growing fast in popularity, and probably not far from official AKC recognition. Agility trials are now held as exhibition-only sports at a few dog shows and always draw big, enthusiastic audiences.

An Agility course, about the size of two or three combined show rings, is set up with obstacles including tunnels, a teeter-totter, an A-frame–type scaling wall, a line of poles to be woven through, a high plank to be walked and an interesting variety of jumps. The game is for the dog to negotiate the whole course, handler running alongside, in the quickest time with the least mistakes. Running time might be, say, forty-five seconds start to finish, over eight jumps, two tunnels, a scaling wall, a swaying bridge, a line of weave poles and a long narrow plank three feet off the ground.

150

It is fun, it is breath-holding excitement, and best of all the dogs love doing it.

Although it is a new sport, if you fall in love with it you can probably find a kennel club or obedience club somewhere within your travel range that has Agility equipment and hosts periodic fun days and trials. You can even make your own equipment.

As with obedience and tracking, most breeds can do Agility, but some do it quite a bit better than others. Still, the Basset Hound that conquers the scaling wall gets wilder applause than the Border Collie, and unlikely breeds are welcomed as warmly as the more traditional Agility breeds.

There are ways of enhancing your enjoyment of the dog world in noncompetitive areas that can give you the necessary balance between aggressive show ring competition and simply owning a pet.

4H—One is working with 4H dog training classes. If you live in or near a rural area it shouldn't be hard to find a county extension office where your offer of assistance with dog training will be welcomed with overwhelming eagerness. The 4H work usually consists of teaching obedience classes for six or eight weeks in early summer, and then putting on the dog show at the county fair. At least that's the way it's done in my area. It may be different where you live.

A few years ago when Agility came on the scene, some of the 4H leaders in this corner of the state began adding Agility to our obedience classes. We built some inexpensive jumps and tunnels, talked the fair boards into letting us experiment, and immediately the dog projects took on new life and excitement. Kids who formerly got bored and dropped out after a year of obedience work were dropping back in and even coming early and staying late on class night.

Nursing Home Visits—Another currently popular way to enjoy our dogs is to share them with nursing home residents. There are organized programs in most places now, usually through the local kennel clubs, that screen dogs for temperament and set up scheduled visits to local nursing homes. Gentle, affectionate dogs love the attention and petting they get, their owners enjoy the feeling of doing some-

Forget any of the downsides of dog shows; THIS is what it's all about.

thing nice, and the nursing home residents derive physical and mental benefits from petting and hugging a warm, waggy dog.

Horse Shows—I know someone who got burned out on dog shows for a while and started spending her weekends taking her beautiful dog to horse shows. Sounds strange, but there was an element of logic in her argument that she loved showing off her dog, and that dog shows were the worst place to do that because they were full of other people wanting to show off their dogs. At horse shows the bleachers were full of animal lovers, as most horse people also liked or loved dogs and appreciated fine, purebred animals. She claimed that she sold more puppies at horse shows than at dog shows, and it might have been true.

Finding Your Own Approaches

If you find yourself incurably addicted to dog shows and yet caught in a love-hate relationship, there are ways to accentuate the positive and downplay, if not eliminate, the negative.

The best defense against dog show blues is that good old sense of humor. Hang on to it, develop it, exercise it every chance you get. It can turn the worst day of your life into a funny story for the next kennel club meeting.

A sense of perspective is equally valuable. None of it is really as important as it seems sometimes. So you got a raw deal, or the judge was brain-dead, or someone is telling nasty lies about you. Big deal. It happens to everybody. Change what you can change, ignore the rest.

As someone once said, you can't lose at a dog show. You can either win or not win, but you cannot lose, because nothing you currently possess can be taken from you. You will either get that juicy two-pointer next Saturday morning, or not get it. You might get it Sunday instead of Saturday, or next week or next month. Win or not win, that's all that's at stake. Nothing you currently possess will be taken from you.

Find ways to indulge yourself. For me the big indulgence was rebuilding my trusty van into a comfortable weekend home and grooming area, with high-rise top, generator for self-sufficiency at any showground, heater and air conditioner for year-round comfort, a good mattress on the bed, a good grooming table and Chopin on the tape player. No more laborious hauling of teetery dollies up and down curbs and through narrow doors. No more fighting for space in overcrowded grooming areas with other people's rock music and noisy children to put up with. Ah, luxury.

This came after woeful experiences with motor homes that broke down continuously, fold-down trailers that took forever to assemble, especially in the rain, and expensive motels that made showing too costly to do very often.

With the camper van I can arrive the day before, get a good location, do my last-minute grooming in comfort and luxury while watching television on Friday night, maybe sleep in Saturday morning and read a book till time to dress and groom. If I win the breed and have to kill three hours till Group time, I can stretch out in my quiet comfortable space, watch TV, read or nap. And if the trip home Sunday night gets too long and late I can pull into a campground for a few dollars and have a good night's sleep without having to exert myself beyond plugging in to the electricity and walking the dogs.

Another way I've expanded my enjoyment of dog show day is by being active in my local kennel club and finding, within that group, my entire circle of friends. A day at the show then becomes a full schedule of grooming and showing my own dogs and watching the rest of the gang, cheering them on and muttering curses with them at their rotten judges or bad luck in obedience.

I know people who only began to enjoy dog shows when they turned their dogs over to professional handlers. For them, the stage-fright outweighed the fun of doing it themselves, but they loved going to the shows and watching their dogs competing. This way, they had all the fun and none of the tension, or at least just enough tension to make it exciting.

We're all different, but we can all find ways to enhance our enjoyment of our dogs. It's up to us as individuals to figure out what we want out of the sport, and what we want to put into it. Dog showing is more than a sport, more than a hobby. It's a life—it's up to you to make it a good one.

ISBN 0-87605-408-4